The Bicycle Repair Book

The Bicycle Repair Book
The complete manual of bicycle care

Rob Van der Plas

Bicycle Books – San Francisco

Copyright © Rob Van der Plas, 1985

92 91 90   10 9 8 7 6

Printed in the United States of America

Published by:
Bicycle Books, Inc., PO Box 2038, Mill Valley CA 94941, USA

Distributed to the book trade by:
USA: The Talman Company,150-5th Ave., New York, NY 10011
UK: Chris Lloyd Sales and Marketing Services, 463 Ashley Rd, Poole BH14 0AX
Canada: Raincoast Book Distr., 112 E-3rd St., Vancouver BC V5T 1C8

Library of Congress Cataloging in Publication Data
Van der Plas, Robert, 1938–
The Bicycle Repair Book
The complete manual of bicycle care
Bibliography: p. Includes index
1. Bicycles and bicycling – Manuals, Handbooks, etc.
2. Authorship – Handbooks, Manuals, etc. I. Title
Library of Congress Catalog Card Number 84-50673

ISBN 0-933201-11-7

About the Author

Rob Van der Plas is a professional engineer and a lifelong bicyclist. Since 1974 he has devoted most of his interest to both bicycle technology and the activity of cycling for sport, recreation and transportation. He has frequently taught courses on the subject of bicycle repair and cycling techniques. His contributions on technical aspects of cycling regularly appear in domestic and foreign bicycle periodicals. In addition to *The Bicycle Repair Book*, he has written *The Mountain Bike Book, The Bicycle Touring Manual, The Bicycle Racing Guide, Roadside Bicycle Repairs* (all published by Bicycle Books), *The Penguin Bicycle Handbook* and numerous other books on bicycle-related subjects, published in Holland, Germany and Denmark.

Table of Contents

1
Know Your Bicycle

This book is devoted entirely to the subject of bicycle care: adjustment, lubrication, maintenance and repairs. Whether you ride a ten-speed, an off-road bike or even a tandem, the instructions are systematically arranged, so that you will find adequate help for all the most frequently encountered problems. They cover not only minor irritations which the experienced cyclist has learned to cope with himself, but also those mysterious things that befuddle even the longtime bicycle rider.

This first chapter is largely an introduction to the bicycle, and is intended primarily for the less experienced rider. If you are quite familiar with the bike and its components, you may wish to skip most of this chapter and go straight on to the more specifically technical matters covered in the chapters that follow. If you are not sure of some of the terminology used in other parts of the book, this is the place to look it up.

Throughout this book I have used American terminology and spelling convention. Thus, my British readers may be somewhat confused, or even offended, to find words like *tire, center* and *aluminum,* where they expect to read *tyre, centre* and *aluminium.* I apologize for this, but it is one of the hard facts of publishing that it is only possible to keep the price of a book down by offering the same version in Britain as in the US. However, I shall make every attempt to refrain as much as possible from using expressions which make sense only on one side of the Atlantic. Wherever the British name for an item differs by more than the spelling alone, I shall provide both terms the first time it is mentioned.

The Parts of the Bicycle

The illustration below shows a ten-speed bicycle, equipped with a full set of accessories. There are many different kinds of bicycles on the road.

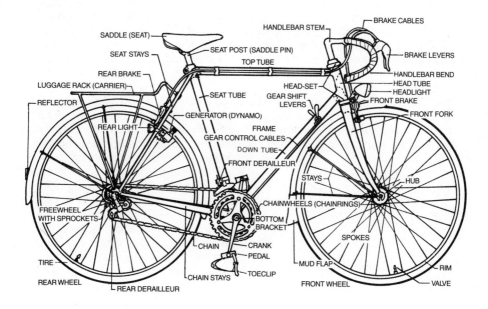

SADDLE (SEAT)
SEAT STAYS
REAR BRAKE
LUGGAGE RACK (CARRIER)
REFLECTOR
REAR LIGHT
SEAT POST (SADDLE PIN)
TOP TUBE
SEAT TUBE
GENERATOR (DYNAMO)
FREEWHEEL WITH SPROCKETS
TIRE
REAR WHEEL
REAR DERAILLEUR
CHAIN STAYS
CHAIN
CRANK
PEDAL
TOECLIP
FRAME
GEAR CONTROL CABLES
DOWN TUBE
FRONT DERAILLEUR
STAYS
CHAINWHEELS (CHAINRINGS)
BOTTOM BRACKET
MUD FLAP
FRONT WHEEL
HANDLEBAR STEM
BRAKE CABLES
BRAKE LEVERS
HANDLEBAR BEND
HEAD TUBE
HEADLIGHT
FRONT BRAKE
FRONT FORK
HUB
SPOKES
RIM
VALVE
HEAD-SET
GEAR SHIFT LEVERS

Many look different from this model and few will be as elaborately equipped. But each of the components shown here can be found on one bike or another. There are of course several distinct bicycle types, which will be briefly described in the next section. First we'll take a look at the various components of the bicycle as shown in the illustration.

The frame is the bicycle's 'backbone'. In fact, it is generally the only part made by the manufacturer whose name appears on the bike: the other parts are bought from specialized suppliers and mounted to the frame in the bicycle manufacturer's plant. The frame is a tubular construction, welded or brazed together to form one structurally sound unit. The tubes of the front portion, or main frame, are top tube, down tube, seat tube and head tube. The rear portion, or rear triangle, consists of two sets of thinner tubes, called chain stays and seat stays respectively. A short tube at the lowest point, where main frame and rear triangle meet, is the bottom bracket shell.

The size of the frame – which should be selected to match the rider's leg length so that he can straddle the top tube with both feet flat on the ground – is usually measured as the total height of the seat tube: from the center of the bottom bracket to the top of the seat tube. An alternative and more precise way, which results in a shorter nominal size for the same actual size frame, is to measure from the center of the bottom bracket to the centerline of the top tube. The latter method is often used on mountain bikes.

The steering system consists of front fork, handlebar, stem and head-set bearings. The head-set bearings are installed in the frame's head tube. The steering system does more than steering alone, because it is also required to balance the bike when going straight.

The wheels are attached to the front fork and the frame. Each wheel consists of hub, spokes, rim and tire. The wheel's nominal size is the diameter measured over the inflated tire. Adult bikes usually have 27-in wheels for ten-speeds or 26-in wheels for mountain bikes, three-speeds and utility bikes. Children's bikes and folding bicycles have smaller wheels. The tire may either be the conventional wired-on type, which consists of separate inner tube and cover, or a tubular racing tire which is cemented to the (special) rim. The latter type is used on racing bicycles only and is called tub in Britain, sew-up in the US.

The drive-train is the set of components that transmits the rider's effort to the rear wheel. It consists of pedals, crankset, chain and sprockets or cogs on the rear wheel. Usually the cogs are mounted on a freewheel mechanism, which may be screwed onto the rear wheel hub or may be integrated into the hub. The crankset consists of cranks, chainwheels and a spindle or axle which runs on the bottom bracket bearings. Often toeclips are installed on the pedals of derailleur bicycles.

The gearing system comes in two distinct versions: derailleur gearing and hub gearing. The former is used almost universally these days – certainly on all ten-speeds and mountain bikes. It consists of a rear derailleur, with which the rider can choose between several different spocket sizes on the freewheel, and often a front de-

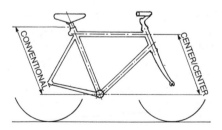

railleur to choose between two or three different front chainwheels.

In the case of hub gearing, a kind of gear box is built into the rear wheel hub. Usually there is a choice of three different gears, although versions with two and five gears are also available. The two-speed hub requires no further control, being operated by pedalling back briefly; all other gear mechanisms are controlled from shift levers via flexible cables. The levers may be mounted on the handlebars, the down tube, the handlebar stem or at the ends of the handlebars. The shifters for hub gears have definite positions representing the various gears, whereas most derailleur gear shifters do not have such fixed positions.

The brakes are most commonly in the form of callipers which squeeze against the rims of the front and rear wheels. There are several different types of such calliper brakes. Other forms of brakes include the coaster brake (also called back-pedalling brake), built into the rear wheel hub, internally expanding hub brakes and the disc brake, as well as the pull-rod operated roller-lever brake (also called stirrup brake). Calliper brakes, drum brakes and disc brakes are generally operated by means of flexible cables.

The saddle is mounted to the frame by means of a seat post, called seat pin or seat pillar in Britain. It is clamped into the bicycle's seat tube by means of a binder bolt which squeezes the split seat lug around the seat post. On mountain bikes this binder bolt usually takes the form of a quick-release device.

Accessories allow the cyclist to optimize his bike for the intended purpose. Some bicycles come equipped with a whole plethora of gadgets, but in the US most are quite devoid of such useful items as lights, fenders (mudguards in Britain), luggage rack, chainguard and pump. Other handy accessories include saddlebag, lock, speedometer, waterbottle and perhaps a warning device, such as a bell or a horn. One item I am less than enthusiastic about, though often installed, is the kick stand (prop stand in Britain).

That's a long list of items, and it's not even remotely complete, because each of these major components itself consists of a number of smaller parts. But such further details will be dealt with in the chapters that follow. For the time being it should suffice if the reader can identify the parts mentioned above on his bicycle. Preferably he should even take the time to 'play around' with them a little, in order to learn how they work and how they are installed.

Bicycle Types

There are several distinct types of bicycles, the most popular of which shall be briefly described here. Quite often the same bike may be referred to by different names, not only by non-cyclists (who will invariably refer to anything with drop handlebars as a 'racing bike', even if it weighs fifty pounds), but even by people in the bicycle business. I shall try to use the most widely used names for each type, mentioning other common names where appropriate.

In addition, it may often be hard to determine whether any particular machine belongs to one category or another, because the distinction sometimes depends on several factors, some of which may indicate a bike is of a particular type, whereas other factors would indicate it belongs to another category. Just the same, most bicycles can be pretty clearly assigned to one of eight basic categories. These shall each be described with an illustration and a few words on the following pages.

Utility bike. This is the traditional American fat-tired fifty-pound monster. In other countries lighter and qualitatively superior machines are in use for the same utilitarian purpose, and the survival of adult transportational cycling in those countries may well be the result of that. The American utility bike has sluggish fat low-pressure tires, flat handlebars, a coaster brake and no gears. Fenders and chainguard are usually installed.

AMERICAN UTILITY BIKE

Ten-speed. This has become the generic term for all bicycles with derailleur gearing and drop handlebars, including machines with anywhere from five to eighteen speeds, and ranging from cheap cash-and-carry junk to racing machines costing over a thousand dollars. Adult sizes almost invariably have 27-in wheels with rather narrow tires. Aluminum alloy components are widely used on the better versions of this type. Accessories are rarely provided on such machines, though in recent years there has been a trend toward equipping some models with good luggage racks and even lights. In Britain and the rest of the civilized bicycle world fenders are generally installed on any model not intended for actual racing.

TEN-SPEED DERAILLEUR BIKE

Three-speed. This is perhaps the best name for what is called roadster in Great Britain. In many parts of the US these bikes are known as English racers: a very inappropriate name indeed, if one considers that this is the British equivalent of the American paperboy bike. Flat handlebars, hub gearing and hand brakes are usually standard. Tires are somewhat narrower than those mounted on the American utility bike. Fenders, chainguard and often a luggage rack are standard accessories.

THREE-SPEED (ROADSTER)

Folding bike. Though rare enough in the US, this bicycle type has long been popular elsewhere. Most of these compromise more desirable qualities in order to achieve stowability. They all have small wheels and are usually equipped with quick-releases for handlebar and saddle adjustments.

FOLDING BIKE

TRACK RACING BICYCLE

Track bike. This is a special racing bicycle for use on a cycle racing track. It has neither gears nor brakes and is extremely light and rigid. The rear wheel is driven directly, without a free-wheel. Like the road racing bicycle, it has very light tubular tires.

Mountain bike. This bike, also known as ATB (all terrain bike) or off-road bike, is a relatively light and so-phisticated bicycle with flat handle-bars and fat high-pressure tires. It is ultimately suitable for use on unsur-faced trails and on poorly surfaced roads and streets. Most have fifteen-speed derailleur gearing. These bikes are particularly suitable for (and popu-lar with) less experienced adult riders, who have never been comfortable with the ten-speed's 'nervousness'.

MOUNTAIN BIKE (ATB)

BMX bike. That's the name for those tiny little agile machines ridden by kids who usually seem big enough to ride a real bicycle. These are the only kids' bikes that differ substantially from most adult bicycles. Not much use for everyday transportation, due to the extremely low gearing; a lot of fun, though, especially off-road.

BMX-BIKE

Tandem. That's a bicycle built for two. It has become increasingly popu-lar in recent years, as qualitatively superior (and very expensive) models have come on the market. Tandems present a number of special mainte-nance problems, most of which will be covered in subsequent chapters of the book.

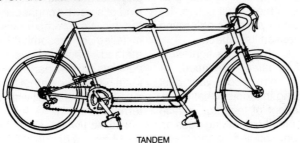

TANDEM

2
The Basics of Bicycle Care

There is more to repairing and maintaining a bicycle than merely following instructions. However systematic the step-by-step guidelines in much of what follows may be, they cannot fully substitute for hands-on experience. Three additional factors will be necessary: the ability to investigate the problem logically, some knowledge of the way basic things like ball bearings and screw threads work, and the ability to handle simple tools.

Applied Thinking

Although I can't teach you to think, I *can* help you by reminding you of the need to do it in the first place. I've known otherwise smart people reduced to utter helplessness when confronted with a simple bicycle problem, not because they were inherently unable to think, but merely because they failed to realize that logical thought, applied to the problem at hand, would have enabled them to solve it. Conversely, there are simple folks who, by applying a kind of logical thinking, quickly establish what is wrong and how to go about correcting the situation.

Don't just think, 'my bike is broken down', but establish just *which* part of the bike is not operating. Consider what the symptoms are. Then, reminding yourself of the way the bike and its major components work, imagine what may be the possible causes. Eliminate them one by one, until you've come to the actual cause. Try to correct it, and if you can't, determine what would lessen its impact.

Consider what must be tightened, adjusted, lubricated, replaced or straightened. Think about your best way of handling the tools: what will fit, what's the effect of leverage, which way to turn, etc. If something does go wrong — a part breaks, a tool slips,

something gets jammed up or damaged — consider what can be done about *that* problem. That's applied thinking.

Also use this kind of applied thinking when confronted with a problem for which you don't seem to have the proper tools. No hammer? Try a brick. Too short? Fit another item over the top. No vice? Find some other method of holding it. There are thousands of simple but ingenious answers to most problems. I can't give you each of these possibilities along with the instructions for doing the job — the book would take on the dimensions of the Gutenberg Bible, if I did. Just use applied thinking, and you will solve almost any problem.

Although this kind of thing is indeed difficult to learn from a book, it's easy enough to develop if you do it consciously, if you remind yourself of the need to do it in the first place. If you consider that the bicycle is still a simple machine, with a limited number of causes of any problem, and if you are aware that it works on easily understood mechanical principles, you can train yourself to think the right way. The remaining factors required for efficient bicycle care — knowing how elementary bicycle components work and how to handle your tools — will be described in rather more detail below.

Nuts and Bolts

This section does not really deal with just nuts and bolts, but rather with any kind of screwed connections. Many of the bicycle's components are either installed or assembled using this method. Each screwed connection consists of two parts: a solid round male part with external threading, and a hollow female part with matching internal threading.

The screw thread is essentially a spiral groove or ridge. Turning the two

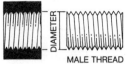

MALE THREAD

FEMALE THREAD

parts relative to one another makes the male part (bolt, screw or threaded axle) wind its way up into the female part (nut or other part with internal threading). If the two parts have clean, undamaged matching threads, this process presents little friction: you can turn them most of the way with little force or leverage.

When I speak of matching threads, I mean that the diameter or nominal size, as well as the other details shown in the illustration (pitch and thread angle), must be the same for both parts. Screw threading on most parts is fairly standardized. On most bicycles (except on low-quality American-built machines) standard metric screw threads are used. So any 6 mm screw will fit any 6 mm nut. On other screwed parts – such as axles and bearing parts – there are some interchangeability problems, which shall be covered below.

Once the two matching parts are screwed so far that they 'bottom out', the slanted sides of the two members' screw threads are pushed together on one side. This causes high friction – enough to hold them in place if adequately tightened and as long as vibration or force does not work to loosen the connection. Only if they are badly worn, and especially when subjected to excessive force or vibration, will they come loose. The threads on very badly worn parts that are forced will actually shear off, so they can not be tightened at all.

Such problems can often be eliminated by means of locking devices. There are several types: lock washers, locknuts, locking inserts and locking adhesives. Several of these methods are used on the bicycle's components as supplied by some manufacturers. It may still be necessary to install a locking device yourself when threaded parts do not remain tight or can not be tightened adequately in the first place.

A lock washer is a serrated or other springy washer that controls the friction force between the female part and whatever is holding it. Even an ordinary plain washer often helps, since it allows you to tighten the parts further before the friction between the seating surfaces becomes so great that the thread cannot do its job properly. For this reason it is advisable to always use a washer under every nut and similar threaded part, especially if one of the parts is of (soft) aluminum.

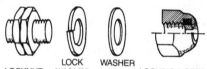

LOCKNUT   LOCK WASHER   WASHER   LOCKING INSERT

A locknut is a second nut, placed on top of or under the regular nut or other part with inside threads. As you tighten the two nuts relative to one another (this time that's usually o.k. without a washer), they'll push against opposite sides of the thread. The resulting balanced force resists the loosening effect of vibration quite effectively. On bearing parts a keyed washer is used between the two parts to prevent incorrect adjustment. Placing a second nut over a regular nut that has tended to come loose – even if perhaps the screw thread is damaged locally – often helps as an emergency repair to hold things together that wouldn't respond to normal tightening.

Locking inserts are sometimes used on vibration-prone small nuts on the bike. They take the form of a somewhat flexible plastic insert in the nut. Replacing ordinary nuts with such locking insert nuts will prevent many things from coming loose. Excellent places to use them are the brake attachments and mountings for accessories, such as fenders, racks and reflectors.

Locking adhesives are sometimes applied to the thread before tightening, if it is a part that must not be tightened, loosened or readjusted frequently. The most familiar trade name is Loctite. There are several types available – get a variety that does not form such a solid bond that you have difficulty breaking it again when you have to loosen the connection later: read the descriptions on the various tubes before you buy.

Always clean screw thread parts before installing, so they are free from rust and dirt, and do not install damaged parts. Use a fine metal wire brush to clean the male thread, then screw it into the female thread a few times before permanently installing, to remove rust and dirt if necessary. Unless you use a locking adhesive, apply lubricant to the screw threads before installing. This retards the formation of rust and prevents direct metal-to-metal contact which might prevent proper tightening, and will ease subsequent loosening or adjusting.

Basic Tools

To tighten or loosen any screwed connection, both the male and the female parts must be held firmly as they are turned relative to one another. To hold such parts firmly, enough leverage and hold is required. Parts that are screwed directly into a threaded hole or onto a threaded boss on the bike require only one tool: the leverage provided when you hold the bike's

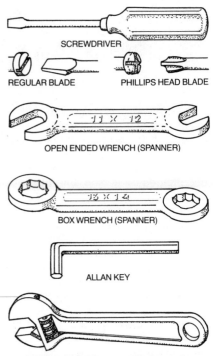

SCREWDRIVER

REGULAR BLADE　　　　PHILLIPS HEAD BLADE

OPEN ENDED WRENCH (SPANNER)

BOX WRENCH (SPANNER)

ALLAN KEY

CRESCENT WRENCH (ADJUSTABLE SPANNER)

frame will be adequate. Screws, nuts, bolts and other small components each require specific tools, which must also be sized to provide the right fit and leverage. Using too big an adjustable tool on a small part may result in too much leverage and force, leading to damage when tightening. Similarly, tools that are too small may not do the job right either. Some types of tools inherently allow more leverage; thus, when tightening a screw-and-nut connection, it will be better to turn the nut with a wrench (high leverage), while holding the screw with the screwdriver (low leverage), than it would be to hold the nut while trying to turn with the screwdriver.

Get several sizes of screwdrivers and two complete sets of other wrenches (called spanners in Britain). The screwdrivers should include at least one small Phillips-head model, one flat blade type with a width of about 3−4 mm (approx. ⅛ in − ⁵⁄₃₂ in), one with a blade width of about 6 mm (¼ in) and one short stubby one with an even wider blade. A big, long screwdriver may come in handy for other jobs, where you use it to get leverage. Always use only properly fitting tools to prevent damage.

The best way of selecting wrenches is to get a set of 6 mm to 16 mm open-ended wrenches and a similar set of box wrenches. In addition, you may get two adjustable wrenches of the type illustrated, called crescent wrenches − I'd say one 6-in long model and a great big one of 8- or 10-in length. The former size can easily be taken along on the bike, the latter one should probably stay in the workshop and doubles as a hand-held vice. Finally, you may have to get some Allen keys: L-shaped hexagonal wrenches to fit the bolts with a hexagonal recess often used on bicycles these days; 4, 5 and 6 mm are the most common sizes, although kickstands may require an 8 mm model and some handlebar stems have a 7 mm recess − get whatever sizes are required for *your* bike.

When selecting tools, consider that only the best will give satisfactory service. Don't be fooled by terms like 'economy tools': such things may be cheap, but they will not be economical in the long run. The best may initially seem expensive, but will save you back the price difference quickly, giving both longer and better service and causing less damage to your bike's components. If you want to economize, do it by selecting tools wisely: only get those tools that are actually required for your bike − you can do without certain sizes. Take your time to establish just which tools, and in which sizes, are required for your bike. This will also help keep the weight down when you take tools along.

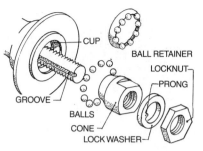

ANGULAR CONTACT (ADJUSTABLE) BEARING

Ball Bearings

Most moving parts of the bicycle run on ball bearings. Although they differ quite a bit in size, they are otherwise similar to one another. The type used almost universally on bicycles is the one illustrated above and is referred to as angular contact bearing or adjustable bearing. The other illustration shows the non-adjustable cartridge bearing, which is used on some components in the highest price class. The latter are not inherently superior, but are often better sealed and require less maintenance. On the other hand, they must be completely replaced when they become loose or fail to run smoothly due to corrosion or after extensive wear. Angular contact bearings, on the other hand, are easily adjusted, lubricated and overhauled by the cyclist himself.

Although I shall give specific instructions for bearing work in each of the descriptions of the following chapters that deal with bearing work, it can not hurt to put you in the picture first. The angular contact bearing consists of two races, referred to as cone and cup respectively, and a set of bearing

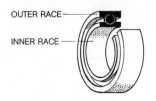

balls. The balls may either lie loose or they may be mounted together in a bearing retainer. Make sure you install that retainer the right way round: so that neither the cone nor the cup touches the body of the retainer. If loose balls are used – and any retainer may be replaced with loose balls of the appropriate size – the balls must be free to move a little; achieve that by installing one ball less than the absolute maximum number that would seem to fit the cup. The space between cup and cone must be generously lubricated, usually with bearing grease, although if you can take the trouble to refill the bearing after every ride, a heavy mineral oil would be even better.

Adjusting a bearing amounts to closing (or opening) the gap between cup and cone slightly. This is done by screwing the appropriate part in or out a little, locking it in place with the locknut or similar device once it is in the right position. The bearings should all be adjusted so that they turn freely without resistance, yet without any noticeable 'play'. To overhaul a bearing, the entire unit is disassembled and any defective parts – always the balls, and also the cup and cone in case they show pits, grooves or corrosion – are replaced. Reassembly is easiest if the cup is first filled with a generous layer of bearing grease to hold the balls in place.

At most locations there is a set of two bearings – one at either end of the axle. Adjusting the one will also affect the other. On some cheaper hubs and on all other bearings only one side is actually adjustable. On pedals that is the outside bearing; on cranks it's the one on the left (i.e. opposite the chain); on the head-set it is the upper bearing.

Bearing work is best done with special tools for the job, which minimize the damage done and ease the work.

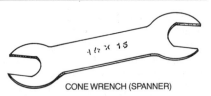

CONE WRENCH (SPANNER)

For wheel bearing adjustment, cone wrenches are used: very thin open-ended wrenches, sold in bike stores. They come in several sizes and you will need two of whatever sizes fit the cones on your bike. Special bearing tools for bottom bracket and head-set work are also available; make sure you get a type that fits the particular makes and models of these components on your bike. Alternately, this work can be done – after a fashion – with improvised tools, as will be explained in the applicable sections of the book.

Control Cables

Derailleurs, hub gears and most brakes are activated by means of Bowden cables. These consist of a flexible metal wire inner cable and a hollow spiral-wound outer cable, which is plastic-coated to keep out dirt and moisture. The outer cable takes up the compressive forces and is anchored at fixed points on the bike; the inner cable takes up tension forces and is attached by means of a nipple at the handle and a clamp bolt at the mechanism to be activated. Cables come in several thicknesses and should be selected with the purpose in mind: brake cables are thicker and have stronger nipples to match the recess in the brake handle. Nipples can take several different forms, so make sure you get the type to match your brake handle or gear shifter.

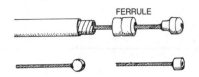

FERRULE

The end of the outer cable is protected by means of a little ferrule; it is usually necessary to cut back the plastic coating locally to install it. The ferrule serves to stop the cable end from slipping inside the anchor point on the bike. Cut off the outer cable (bought by the running foot) so that no hook is formed at the end, because that would interfere with the free movement of the inner cable. The cable must be long enough, and routed so that no 'kinks' are formed anywhere (replace cables that are damaged this way). The inner cable must be cut off so that the end does not fray; it is best to solder the strands together at the end where it is cut off, since frayed ends make adjustment or reinstallation impossible and may lead to injury. Replace inner cables that are frayed anywhere except at the end protruding from the clamp. Allow the inner cable some excess length, to make it easier to adjust while holding it taut with pliers – at least an inch should protrude.

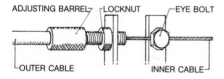

In many cases a barrel adjuster is installed somewhere in the cable to make adjustment of the cable tension easy. Hold the adjuster with one hand while loosening the locknut; then screw the adjuster in or out as appropriate; finally, hold the adjuster again, while tightening the locknut. Some other cables, such as those used on the brakes of mountain bikes, may rely on a simple knurled round adjusting nut built into the handle. When the range of the adjuster has been taken up completely, readjust the clamping position of the cable on the mechanism. Screw the adjuster in as far as it will go, then loosen the clamp bolt, pull the cable taut with a wrench or pliers, and tighten the clamp bolt. Fine adjustments are then again made with the barrel adjuster or the adjusting nut on the handle.

Soldering

Electrical wire ends are more reliable and control cable ends do not fray when they are soldered. Use an electric soldering iron with an output of at least 60 watt and rosin core soldering wire. Clean the wire ends and any contact before soldering. Heat the metal to be joined with the soldering iron, then add the soldering wire while still holding soldering iron and connection together. Let the liquified soldering material penetrate the joint. Finally hold the contact in place while removing the heat source, waiting for it to cool (the soldering metal on the joint becomes dull) before you let go of it. In addition to control cable ends, you can solder contact eyes to electric wires and solder together the strands of the copper wire to stop them from fraying and to provide a better contact.

Seat and Handlebar Adjustment

For safe, comfortable and efficient cycling, the correct positions of saddle and handlebars are critically important. Once these are correctly established, mark them by engraving the handlebar stem and the seat post to reflect this position for quick adjustment when the bike has been disassembled or readjusted for any reason. If you're still growing – that may be up to age 22 – these things must be checked and corrected regularly, say every two months. In that case, mark the position with adhesive tape, instead of engraving. Whenever you ride another bike, it will be a great help if you can quickly determine the correct positions and carry out these adjustments before you hop onto it. Pro-

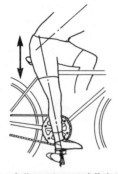

ceed as follows to establish the correct fit, then follow the instructions in Chapters 4 and 5 for *Handlebar Adjustment* and *Saddle Adjustment* respectively.

To establish the correct seat height, place one pedal in the lowest position, holding the bike close to a post or a wall from which you can support yourself. Wear shoes without heels (e.g. cycling shoes, slippers or light sneakers). Now mount the bike, leaning against the post or the wall to keep yourself and the bike perfectly vertical. Reach down for the pedal with the heel of the foot. The leg should be almost stretched, with just a little 'play' left in the knee joint. Now pedal backward to establish whether you are indeed sitting straight: you should not have to rock from side to side when pedalling. On bikes with a coaster brake, pedalling backward is not possible; in that case you'll have to do a little actual cycling in this position to make sure you're sitting right. Once you cycle properly, you should *not* keep the heel of the foot on the pedal – then the ball of the foot (the second joint of the big toe) must lie over the center of the pedal. For adjustments see Chapter 5.

To find the correct forward position of the saddle, place the pedals in the horizontal position. Now measure with an improvised plumb line (e.g. a big nut or bolt on a piece of twine) whether the knee joint of the forward leg is ver-

tically above the pedal axle. Again, details for correction can be found in Chapter 5. The top of the saddle should also be close to horizontal; this adjustment, too, is described in Chapter 5.

Now for the handlebars, take a look at the illustration, which shows a 'relaxed' riding posture. The highest point of the handlebars should be as high as, or slightly lower than, the top of the saddle. The distance between saddle and handlebars should be such that your body roughly forms a triangle as shown, with the arms slightly bent at the elbows and the shoulders roughly midway between saddle and handlebars. This is a relaxed position, which allows for variation during actual cycling by holding the handlebars in a different position (in the case of drop or 'racing' bars). If you ride a mountain bike or another

model with flat handlebars, adjustments to your posture for increased
power or reduced wind resistance are
not so easy to make. On mountain
bikes you may have to temporarily
lower the saddle with its quick-release
during a steep descent. However, for
normal riding this position of saddle
and handlebars is about optimal.
Height adjustments of the handlebars
are covered in Chapter 4; the distance between saddle and handlebars is varied by means of replacing
the handlebar stem by one with a
different length.

Lubrication

Lubrication is needed to minimize
friction and to prevent wear and damage of the bicycle's moving parts.
But don't just pour oil or smear grease
in and around the bike's moving parts:
lubrication and cleaning should go
hand in hand – clean and lubricate
selectively, then wipe off any excess
lubricant. Excess lubricants attract
dirt and moisture, and this mixture
only makes things worse.

The ultimate lubricant for most
parts is mineral oil (e.g. motor oil).
Unfortunately, bicycles are no longer
equipped with oiling nipples,so that
they must now mainly be lubricated
with grease. That's relatively easy,
because grease stays in place longer
than oil. However, it does require disassembly of parts that could otherwise be left alone. At least once a year
all bearings should be disassembled
and refilled with bearing grease. The
chain should be washed out in solvent
and then immediately lubricated perhaps four times a year – more often if
you cycle in bad weather; details in
Chapter 6. Chain lubricant and bearing
grease can be bought at bike stores or
motorcycle stores; oil and bearing
grease are readily available at hardware and automotive parts stores as
well.

Most other parts of the bike are
probably best lubricated with the thin
penetrating kind of mineral oil that
comes in spray cans, such as WD-40
or the lightest form of LPS. Use it with
the tubular nozzle that is supplied
with the spray can, to aim as accurately as possible. Treat all the various
privots of the bicycle's mechanisms,
as well as the points where cables
disappear into outer cables, this way.
Before you lubricate, clean these
parts and the area affected with a dry
rag or brush; wipe excess lubricant off
when you've finished.

Cleaning the Bike

To keep the bicycle operating properly,
it may be enough to merely clean and
lubricate the moving parts as described above. However, a complete cleaning job will not only keep the bike looking pretty, it will also increase its life
and makes for more pleasant riding,
handling and maintaining. I suggest
doing this work at least four times a
year – more often if you ride a lot in
inclement weather and in dusty or
muddy terrain. Here's how you go
about it.

1. Wipe off any loose dirt with a rag
or a soft brush. The most suitable
brushes for all cleaning jobs are the
cylindrical so-called bottle brushes;
get two different sizes – a big one and
a smaller one that fits in the smallest
nooks and crannies.

2. Wash off any remaining dirt with a
wet rag or brush, rinsing it out in
plenty of water. Greasy dirt will come

off better when you use water and soap, then rinse with water. Try not to get water in the bearings of the bike's moving parts (wheel axles, pedals, bottom bracket, head-set) and on the saddle, especially if it is a real leather one.

3. Remove any really persistent greasy dirt, using a mixture of kerosene (that's called paraffin in Britain) and about one part in ten of motor oil. You can use any other solvent, even without mixing in the oil, providing you immediately wipe if off to prevent the formation of rust. Alternately, spray on special cleaning oil or lubricant, and rub off with a clean rag.

4. Take particular care to clean in hard-to-get-at places, like between the chainwheels and inside brakes and derailleurs.

5. If necessary, remove any corrosion of blank metal parts, using metal polish, and of scratched or chipped painted surfaces with sandpaper.

6. Lubricate, using the lubricants suggested, according to the instructions in the preceding section, all pivot points and the points where inner cables disappear into outer cables or guides.

7. With a soft clean cloth, spread acid-free vaseline on the blank metal parts, except the rims' braking surfaces. Paintwork may be protected with car wax; however, if there are scratched and chipped areas which you have sandpapered, these must be touched up with paint, using a small brush first (see Chapter 12), and then allowed to dry at least 24 hours before you apply wax.

Note: For this and many other jobs, the wheels should be raised off the ground, eg with the aid of a simple display stand. Some other jobs are best done when the bike is raised higher off the ground on a special repair stand or placed upside down. In the latter case, place it on a home-built handlebar support to avoid damage to cables and controls. Instructions to build repair supports are contained in Chapter 13.

Regular Maintenance Check

The instructions in this book do not only cover repairs, but also preventive maintenance: not only things to do when the bike breaks down, but also things to do in order to prevent breakdowns before they develop. I suggest three levels of maintenance checks at different time intervals to keep your bike in optimal condition. Here follows a very rough outline of these checkups. Refer to the appropriate sections of the book for detailed instructions as to just how these various jobs can best be performed. Just don't neglect 'instant maintenance', though: repair anything you notice between checkups as soon as you can.

Daily check-up. Do this work before you get on the bike each day you ride it. It takes only a couple of minutes to perform, but could well save your life; at a minimum it will asure your ride is as efficient, safe and comfortable as possible.

1. Check the brakes for effectiveness; adjust if necessary.

2. Check the tire pressure; inflate if necessary; take the pump along.

3. Check whether the wheels turn freely and are held firmly in the frame.

4. Check whether saddle and handlebars, brake handles and shift levers are in their proper positions and properly tightened.

5. If you may be riding in the dark, make sure your lights are installed and operating.

Monthly check-up. That's what I call it, but if you ride in bad weather a lot, it may be advisable to do it more frequently. First clean and lubricate the bike according to the instructions given in the preceding sections of this chapter, then proceed as follows, referring to the detailed instructions in the remaining chapters wherever necessary.

1. Check all nuts, bolts and other attachments (including specifically those of cranks and chainwheels); tighten or replace anything that is not fastened properly.

2. Check whether the wheels are true (i.e. don't seem to wobble sideways as they are turned) and the spoke tension is evenly high on all spokes on the same side of each wheel.

3. Check whether the wheels line up and that there is no frame or fork damage. See Chapters 3 and 4 for instructions.

4. With the bicycle on a repair stand or upside-down (taking the precautions mentioned above), check the tires for sharp embedded objects, wear or damage, making any necessary correction or replacement as described in Chapter 9, *The Wheels.*

5. Check and, if necessary, adjust the bearings of wheel hubs, crank-set and pedals, following the instructions in the appropriate chapters.

6. Check the operation of the gears, and make any adjustments necessary, as outlined in Chapter 7 or 8.

7. Check the brake shoes of rim brakes for correct alignment and wear; adjust or replace if necessary, as described in Chapter 10.

8. Check the chain for wear and tension, as outlined in Chapter 6.

9. Put the bike back 'on its feet' and correct any problems that may still exist, as evidenced in a test ride, using all the gears and the brakes consciously and critically.

10. Check the contents of your repair kit and first aid kit, to make sure they are complete.

Biannual check-up. At least that's what it should be if you ride both in winter and in summer. If you only use the bike in summer, this work should at least be done at the *end* of the season; in that case, do another monthly check at the beginning of the next season. I'll refrain from step-by-step instructions for this: just do everything listed for the monthly check-up and, in addition, clean and lubricate the chain, overhaul all bearings, replace and lubricate all cables, and carry out all other jobs that may seem appropriate, such as replacing the handlebar tape. This is also the time to touch up scratched paint and to replace older tubes and worn tire covers.

3
The Frame

In this and subsequent chapters the major component groups will be treated. For each of these a brief section will describe the component itself, after which the various repairs and maintenance jobs are outlined.

As far as repair work is concerned, not too much usually goes wrong with the frame. It is merely treated first because it *is* the bicycle's major component: a bike without a wheel, a crank or a saddle is still a bike, but without a frame you just haven't a bike, but rather a bunch of odd parts.

The frame forms the backbone of the bicycle. It consists of a tubular assembly as shown in the illustration. The illustrated frame is the most typical form, on which the tubes are joined by means of lugs into which the ends of the tubes are brazed. Some frames don't have lugs; such lugless frames are either brazed directly without lugs, or they are welded together. See the illustration for the terminology. In addition, some frames have several minor attachments brazed onto the tubes.

The size of the frame is measured by one of the two methods shown on page 10. Other critical dimensions are the total length or wheelbase, and the clearances for the wheels. To replace a damaged frame, it will be ne-

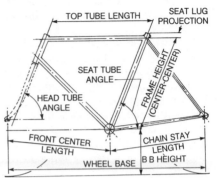

cessary to check these dimensions, as well as the simple nominal frame size, especially if the bike has a non-standard wheel size, standard here meaning 27 in or 700 mm (nominal: their actual diameter is only about 680 mm or slightly less than 27 in) for the wheels of ten-speed bikes, 26 in for mountain bikes and most other types. When replacing a frame, also note my remarks about different threading standards etc. for head-sets, bottom brackets and derailleur mounts.

Prices and weights for complete frames can vary dramatically, depending on the kind of materials used and the care that has gone into building it. In general, within any particular bicycle category, lighter means more expensive. Due to the choice of supe-

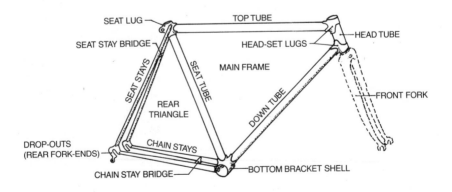

rior materials, lighter frames can still be as strong as the cheaper, heavy models. The lightest frames are built with seamless drawn steel alloy tubing, whereas simpler and heavier machines have frames made of simple (and inherently weaker) welded carbon steel tubing. The very lightest frames use butted tubing for the main tubes, on which the ends have a slightly greater wall thickness than the rest of the tube. The label on the frame usually tells you what kind of tubing was used. To check whether a frame is made of seamless tubing or not, you can feel inside the bottom bracket into the downtube to establish whether a weld seam is present. This is no unnecessary precaution, because I have several times found that some manufacturers were cheating, selling a frame with a sticker that proclaimed it was made of butted tubing, whereas I could establish it was merely welded tubing: nothing seamless, let alone butted. There's no way of checking for wall thickness differences (butting), short of cutting up the frame.

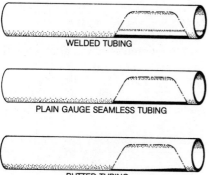

A good frame is perfectly straight, i.e. symmetrical with respect to a plane drawn through the centerlines of the main tubes. That will be one of the major maintenance checks described below. Other things that may go wrong with the frame vary from big problems, like broken tubes, to minor things, like scratched paint (covered in Chapter 12). Perhaps the most frequent cause of frame damage is insufficient care when transporting the bike. Minimize this risk by placing blocks or similar items between the drop-outs when the wheels are removed – a set of old hubs is perfect for this purpose.

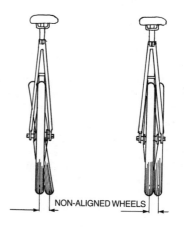

NON-ALIGNED WHEELS

Frame Inspection

When the bicycle is not 'tracking' properly, i.e. when it seems to take too much effort to steer and balance it, or when it tends to vibrate or wobble when riding at speed, either the wheels, the steering system or the frame are the cause. Before tackling the frame, check whether the wheels are aligned by looking from behind, as shown in the illustration. Check whether the wheels are each perfectly true and centered, and whether the bearings are properly adjusted, as described in Chapter 9. Then check whether the fork is straight and the head-set is adjusted properly, as described in Chapter 4. Only after you have ascertained that all these factors are correct, should you start to suspect frame alignment. Proceed as follows:

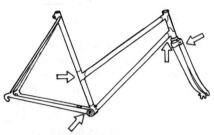

TYPICAL FRAME DAMAGE LOCATIONS

Tools and equipment:
☐ 10–12 ft of twine
☐ callipers (in Britain: vernier gauge)
☐ straightedge

Procedure
1. Check the locations indicated in the illustration above for damage, such as bulges or cracks. Any frame so damaged should be handled by a bike mechanic, who may tell you the frame can be repaired. At any rate, that's not a job you can tackle yourself.

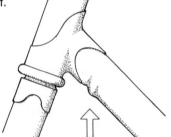

2. Wrap the twine around the frame as shown, pulling the ends taut beyond the drop-outs. Now compare the distance between the twine and the seat tube on both sides. Unless this is a special frame with an off-set to allow the use of a centered (undished) rear wheel (very rare indeed, and if it were, you'd probably know about it), these two distances should measure the same to within ± 1.5 mm (1⁄16 in). If not, your frame is warped. Have a bike mechanic straighten it for you, or proceed in accordance with the instruction *Cold Setting* below.

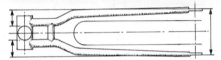

MEASURE ALONG STRAIGHTEDGE
TO VERIFY SYMMETRY

3. Place the straightedge on the RH drop-out and measure the distance between it and the seat tube. Do the same on the LH side. The two must again be identical to within ± 1.5 mm (1⁄16 in). If they're not, see your friendly bike mechanic or follow the instruction *Straighten Drop-outs* below.

4. Measure the distance between the outsides of the two drop-outs. Now compare this to the sum of the distances measured under point 3 and the diameter of the seat tube. If these distances are not identical to within 1.5 mm (1⁄16 in), the drop-outs must also be straightened as described below.

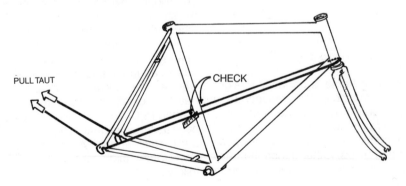

PULL TAUT   CHECK

Cold Setting

The way bent frames are straightened is politely referred to as cold setting: bending them back straight without heating. That may sound crude, but it's essentially the same method used by professionals, who of course use more sophisticated tools and measuring equipment, though the principle is the same. If you're not of a nervous nature, you may try doing it yourself, except if your frame is one of the most expensive models, since in that case the risk of doing damage is much greater, due to the very light tube gauge used. This is how you go about it, after you have established in the preceding check what exactly is the nature of your problem, and know just how much you have to bend which part in which direction.

Nine times out of ten, the problem with a misaligned frame is caused by the rear triangle (seat and chain stays). It is possible that the seat tube and the head tube do not lie in the same plane, but it's unlikely and hard to correct. Besides, bending the rear triangle may correct adequately to compensate for the effect of this kind of misalignment as well. The thinner tubes of the rear triangle are easier to bend – both unintentionally, causing the problem in the first place, and intentionally, to correct it again. So that's what I'll describe here. No special tools will be required for this job.

1. First establish exactly how far each half of the rear triangle has to be bent out and in which direction, based on both the over-locknut dimension of the rear hub and the alignment check described above.

2. Place the frame on a strong table or a similar level area, the rear triangle protruding over the edge. I like to use the front porch, except for the public attention it draws to the crudeness of this operation. Get a friend to stand on

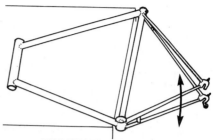

COLD SETTING: BEND TO STRAIGHTEN

the frame at the head tube and the seat tube.

3. Bend the side that's facing up in or out until the correct position has been reached, comparing the distance between the lower and the upper drop-outs before and after bending.

4. Turn the frame over and do the same with the other rear triangle. When you've finished, the distance between the drop-outs should be identical to the over-locknut width of the rear hub.

5. Carry out the alignment check described above and make any corrections that may be necessary.

Straighten Drop-outs

Drop-outs or fork-ends, as they are called in Britain, should be parallel and straight. If they aren't, as established in the description *Frame Inspection* above, they can usually be bent back without doing serious damage quite easily. No step-by-step instruction here: just place a crooked drop-out in the jaws of the vice over its

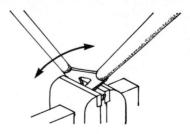

entire length and, using the frame for leverage, bend it back into shape. If you don't have a vice, let someone else hold the frame and, using a big adjustable wrench, set for the exact thickness of the drop-out, bend the thing back. If the wrench gives insufficient leverage, you may fit a piece of tube (water pipe or whatever) over the top of the handle. If the drop-out itself is not straight, use two wrenches or a wrench and a vice, one on either side of the bend, to correct the situation. Always check again when you've finished and make any corrections that may be called for. If noticeable cracks

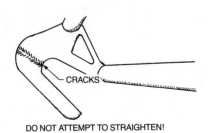

DO NOT ATTEMPT TO STRAIGHTEN!

have developed, or if the drop-out is seriously bent out, it may be necessary to have the entire drop-out replaced: go and see a bike mechanic about a job like that.

4
The Steering System

The steering system consists of the front fork, the handlebars with their extension or stem, and the head-set bearings. The fork may also be considered part of the frame, since it is usually sold together with it – the combination of frame and fork is referred to as frame set. As was briefly mentioned in Chapter 1, the steering system is also required to keep the bike on a straight course and to allow balancing.

Repair and maintenance work on the steering system most typically takes the form of adjusting or overhauling the head-set bearings. After some serious abuse or a crash the fork may be bent or even broken, in which case it must be replaced (or straightened by someone who knows how to do it, if it's bent in a less critical place). In addition, I will describe the various minor operations, such as adjustments and replacement of the handlebars and the stem.

Let's first take a look at the complete assembly. The whole system pivots around the head-set bearings. These are held with a press fit in the frame's head tube. The fork is held inside these bearings, the upper one of which is adjustable on the steerer tube (also called fork shaft). The handlebars are held in the fork shaft with a clamping device at the bottom of the handlebar stem. Usually the stem and the handlebars are two separate units, in which case the handlebar stem is also referred to as extension or goose-neck. A clamping device then holds the handlebars in the stem. Drop handlebars are usually covered by wrapping handlebar tape around them; most other bars use handgrips at the ends.

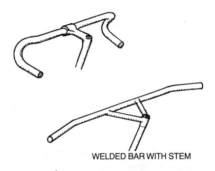

WELDED BAR WITH STEM

Handlebars and Stem
Handlebars come in many different shapes and sizes. They can be assigned to one of the following categories: drop bars (as used on racing bikes), flat bars (as used on mountain bikes) and raised bars (as used on many three-speeds and utility bikes). Sometimes it may be desirable to modify the shape of the bars to the rider's preference. I've seen racing bars spread out, turned over and cut short, and I've seen upright bars used upside-down and flat bars cut off at the ends. No instructions for this kind of work: use your own ingenuity, a hacksaw and whatever else seems to be required. After a crash it may be necessary to do the same to straighten out a handlebar; just make sure there are no cracks!

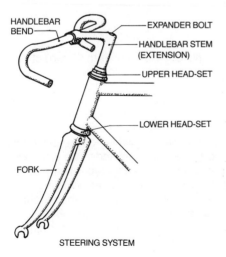

HANDLEBAR BEND

EXPANDER BOLT

HANDLEBAR STEM (EXTENSION)

UPPER HEAD-SET

LOWER HEAD-SET

FORK

STEERING SYSTEM

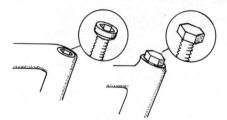

For interchangeability it is worth noting the dimensional conventions. Most critical are the diameter of the stem and the diameter of the handlebar bend at the point where it is clamped inside the stem. These dimensions are given in mm, and should be measured with callipers (vernier gauge) to ensure a correct fit. Stems made to French dimensions have a slightly smaller outside diameter than most other stems. Consequently, a non-French stem may be too tight to fit in a French front fork steerer tube, whereas it's a bit loose the other way round. Most handlebars with separate stems have a center section diameter of 25, 26 or 26.5 mm; make sure the two parts match, though at a pinch you can add a shim cut from an aluminum beverage can. Some cheaper American built bikes and some models of other big manufacturers, such as the original British Raleigh company (not to be confused with the American company with the same name, which is actually part of Huffy and has nothing but the name in common with the original Raleigh), use items that only fit their own bikes – that's where it pays to measure very carefully and to make sure you are aware which makes of bike and components you're dealing with.

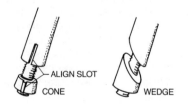

ALIGN SLOT
CONE
WEDGE

Handlebar Height Adjustment

How the correct handlebar height is determined was briefly described in Chapter 2. To make the actual adjustment, proceed as follows:

Tools and equipment
□ wrench to fit expander bolt (depending on the type of bolt, this may be either an Allen key or any type of wrench for a hexagonal bolt head)
□ hammer or mallet (also a piece of wood to protect the bolt head if you use a steel hammer)

Procedure
1. Loosen the expander bolt by at least four turns.
2. Hold the bike with the front wheel off the ground, supporting the handlebars, then hit the head of the expander bolt sharply to loosen the internal wedge or cone.
3. Move the handlebars in the desired position and tighten the expander bolt again, making sure the bars are straight.

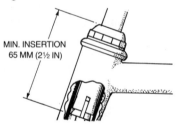

MIN. INSERTION
65 MM (2½ IN)

Note: At least 65 mm (2½ in) of the stem should remain inside the steerer tube. Some stems have a marking engraved to show the maximum protrusion consistent with this requirement. If yours is not marked this way, it may be worthwhile to take the stem out, measure it up and make your own marking. If the handlebars cannot be raised enough without violating this requirement, you should shop around for a stem with a longer shaft, and replace it according to the appropriate instructions below.

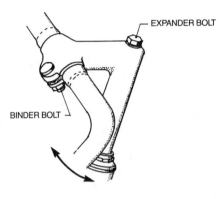

EXPANDER BOLT

BINDER BOLT

Handlebar Angle Adjustment
This adjustment is only possible on handlebars with a separate stem.

Tools and equipment
☐ wrench to fit the nut on the binder bolt which clamps the handlebar bend in the stem.

Procedure
1. Loosen the nut on the binder bolt about one half to one turn.
2. Turn the handlebar bend in the desired orientation, making sure it is still centered with respect to the stem.
3. Tighten the nut on the binder bolt again.
Note: Some (usually expensive) stems have a special 'hidden' binder bolt underneath the stem; such items are invariably operated with an Allen key, as are some models that are otherwise conventional.

Replace Handlebar Bend or Stem
You will want to replace the handlebars if they are seriously bent or otherwise damaged, or when you are unhappy with their size, shape or appearance. The same instructions are followed if the stem is replaced. This description covers handlebars with a separate stem; for handlebars with a welded-on stem, refer to the instructions for replacing bars and stem.

Tools and equipment
☐ wrench to fit nut on stem binder bolt
☐ large screwdriver
☐ any tools required to remove brake levers and whatever else is mounted on the handlebars (see appropriate instructions elsewhere in the book)

Procedure
1. Remove any cables and other connections on the handlebar, as well as the brake lever, the handlebar tape or handgrips, and whatever else may be mounted on the handlebars *on one side.*
2. Leaving the stem attached to the bike, unscrew the binder bolt nut and remove the binder bolt.
3. Pry open the binder clamp on the stem with the big screwdriver, while pushing the thicker center section of the bend out of it, working towards the side without tape or grip. Do this carefully so as not to scratch the finish if the bend is meant to be used again.
4. To reinstall or replace, again open up the clamp and, taking the same care as before, put the new bend in place.
5. Check the position and angle accurately and tighten the binder bolt firmly. If it cannot be tightened adequately to prevent the bars from slipping (could be very dangerous when braking), you will need a bar with a larger outside diameter or, conversely, a stem with a smaller clamp diameter, unless a shim as shown here – cut from an aluminum beverage can – will do the trick.

USE SHIM IF BAR TOO NARROW

Replace Handlebars with Stem

This work will be necessary whenever the head-set has to be overhauled or replaced and when the fork is to be removed. Of course, it is also required to replace the stem or the complete handlebar unit.

Tools and equipment

□ wrench to fit expander bolt
□ hammer or mallet (when using a steel hammer: also a block of wood to protect the head of the bolt)
□ any tools that may be needed to remove the various items mounted on the handlebars – do that work before starting to remove the handlebars

Procedure

1. Unscrew the expander bolt by at least four turns.

2. Hold the bike with the front wheel off the ground, supporting the handlebars, then hit the head of the expander bolt sharply to loosen the internal wedge or cone.

3. Pull the stem out of the fork shaft, if necessary in a twisting motion.

4. To reinstall, first make sure the wedge or cone at the bottom of the stem is seated properly. The ribs on the cone must lie in the slots in the stem, but the expander bolt must be loose enough to allow for easy insertion of the stem inside the steerer tube.

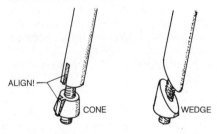

5. Insert the stem to the right height. At least 65 mm (2½ in) must be inside the steerer tube – mark the stem correspondingly if it is not so marked by the manufacturer.

6. Holding the bar in the correct position, tighten the expander bolt.

Reverse-Thrust Expander Bolt

This clever device – first introduced by the British manufacturer GB on the unique Moulton sprung bicycles in 1983, but now also available for regular bikes – dispenses with hammering to remove or loosen the handlebar stem. The head of the expander bolt is recessed further into the stem, and this recess is partially closed in the top with a circlip (a flat spring insert, roughly in the shape of a horseshoe). The Allen key to release the expander bolt is inserted through the center of the circlip into the head of the bolt. After the bolt has been unscrewed a few turns its head pushes from the back against the inside of the circlip, and the reverse thrust of this action pushes the cone at the end off the bolt. Three or four more turns will allow you to remove or adjust the stem.

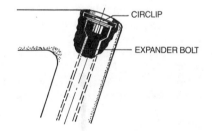

Install Handlebar Tape or Handgrips

Handlebar tape comes in several versions: self-adhesive cotton, leather, cork, felt and plastic. In addition, there are foam sleeves and handgrips. The latter are easier to install and remove if they are either submerged in hot water first, or when a drop of liquid detergent (dishwashing liquid) is applied between the grip and the handlebars first. The following instructions apply to the installation of handlebar tape.

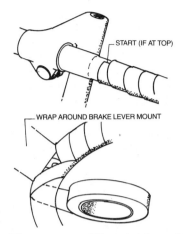

START (IF AT TOP)

WRAP AROUND BRAKE LEVER MOUNT

There are two different philosophies on the correct way of installing tape: starting at the top and starting at the bottom, respectively. If you start at the bottom, clamp the beginning between the end of the handlebars and the handlebar plug, and hold the end with adhesive tape. If you start at the top, you only need a piece of adhesive tape at the beginning if you use non-adhesive tape. Either way, wrap the tape around the brake handles as shown. Make sure the brake handles are installed in the correct position before you start wrapping. The other illustration shows the two different kinds of bar-end plugs. The screw-clamp type must be loosened before it is installed, then tightened with a screwdriver.

If you use bar-end gear shift levers, the control cables are either run under the tape or through the handlebars. Decide where exactly the cable should be routed so that it interferes the least

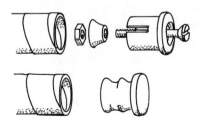

with your holding the bars, and tape it down in that position. The shifters themselves are installed according to the instructions in Chapter 7, *Derailleur Gearing.*

The Head-Set

The illustration shows the parts of a typical head-set. A few models differ slightly, but the instructions below will still be adequate guidance even for those oddballs. The head-set consists of two bearings, one at each end of the head tube. The fixed bearing cups are installed with a press fit into the ends of the head tube. Note that there are differences between French standard dimensions and almost everybody elses, (English and Italian standards are close enough to allow 'mixing' without serious damage).

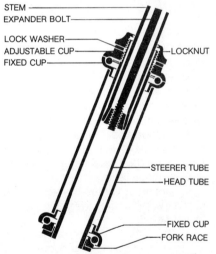

STEM
EXPANDER BOLT
LOCK WASHER
ADJUSTABLE CUP
FIXED CUP
LOCKNUT
STEERER TUBE
HEAD TUBE
FIXED CUP
FORK RACE

If the cup is too tight or too loose, you have the wrong type for the frame in question. Similarly, the screw thread must match that on the fork shaft. Here's how to adjust a head-set that is too loose or too tight – it should turn smoothly but without noticeable play. The other instruction deals with a complete overhaul of the head-set; it must also be followed to replace a head-set or a front fork.

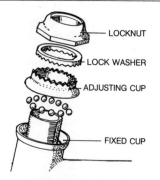

- LOCKNUT
- LOCK WASHER
- ADJUSTING CUP
- FIXED CUP

Adjust Head-Set

The head-set must be adjusted if the steering does not operate smoothly or when it is obviously too loose. If the bike vibrates at speed, one possible reason may be a loose head-set. If adjusting does not help, or if adjusting aggravates another problem, the entire head-set must be overhauled or replaced.

Tools and equipment
□ big wrench to fit locknut and adjustable race on upper head-set bearing

Procedure
1. Unscrew locknut until the lock washer can be lifted perceptibly (if the lock washer and the underlying adjustable race have teeth, as shown in the illustration, it must be lifted enough to clear those teeth).
2. Loosen or tighten the adjustable cup as appropriate, then tighten the locknut again.
3. Check the operation of the steering system once more and make any further adjustments that may be necessary the same way, until the steering is neither stiff nor loose.

Overhaul or Replace Head-Set

When adjusting does not do the trick, or when the fork or the head-set must be removed or replaced for other reasons, follow these instructions, after the handlebars have been removed.

Tools and equipment
□ big wrench to fit locknut and adjustable race on upper head-set bearing
□ to remove fixed cups: special tool or large screwdriver
□ to remove fork race: special tool or medium size screwdriver
□ to remove or install fixed cup: special tool or hammer; block of wood
□ to install fork race: special tool or hammer; piece of 1¼ diameter tubing, slightly longer than the steerer tube
□ rag
□ bearing grease

Note: Although the use of provisional tools is illustrated, special tools are preferable. Work very carefully when using provisional tools.

Procedure
1. Unscrew locknut on upper head-set bearing.
2. Lift off lock washer.
3. Unscrew adjustable bearing race.
4. Remove the fork from the head tube, catching the bearing balls

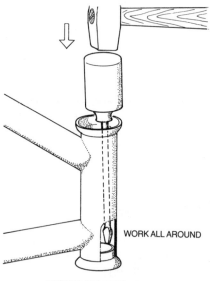

WORK ALL AROUND

BEARING CUP REMOVAL

(usually contained in retainers) from the top and bottom head-set bearings.

5. Inspect all parts – do not reuse any bearing part that is grooved, pitted or corroded. Always replace the bearing balls.

6. If the fixed cups must be replaced, remove and install as shown in the illustration. Make sure to use only parts that fit correctly.

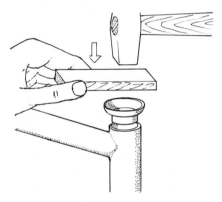

BEARING CUP INSTALLATION

7. If the fork race is to be replaced, remove and install as shown in the illustrations. It may be necessary to file the step on the fork crown that holds the fork race down a little if the fit is too tight; if, on the other hand, the fit is too loose, you must get a race that fits properly.

8. Clean all bearing surfaces, then fill both cups with bearing grease.

9. Holding the bike upside-down, install the bearing balls in the lower cup. If you use loose bearing balls (usually size $5/32$ in) use one ball less than the absolute maximum number that would seem to go in. If you use a ball retainer, make sure it is installed so that only the balls touch the two races – not the cage.

10. Install the fork, turn over the bike, and place the bearing balls in the upper race, following the same precautions as for point 9 above.

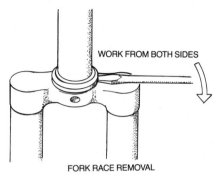

WORK FROM BOTH SIDES

FORK RACE REMOVAL

11. Install the adjustable cup, followed by the lock washer and the locknut.

12. Adjust the head-set for smooth operation without undue play in the bearings, following the procedure *Adjust Head-Set* above.

Note: Should it still be impossible to get satisfactory operation, the fork's steerer tube may be bent. See the procedure below.

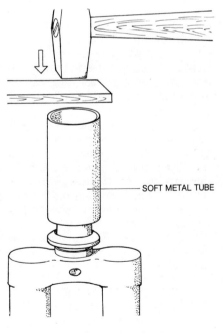

SOFT METAL TUBE

FORK RACE INSTALLATION

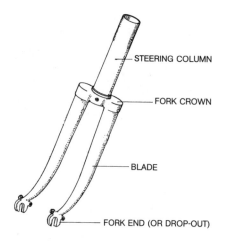

STEERING COLUMN

FORK CROWN

BLADE

FORK END (OR DROP-OUT)

The Front Fork

The front fork consists of a steerer tube (or fork shaft), a fork crown, two fork blades and, at the end of the fork blades, fork-ends or drop-outs. The fork blades are bent forward by a certain distance, referred to as rake. When the cyclist hits an unmovable object – whether this be a tree, a curbstone or a rain gutter in the road – the front fork is the most likely part of the bike to be damaged: the fork blades will get bent back. Other forms of damage are a bent steerer tube, which will be noticed if the steering becomes stiff, a broken steerer tube (there's no way you can fail to notice that, if you survive the accident) or sideways misalignment of the fork blades, which is often the result of careless transportation of the bike. The last problem is avoided by installing an old hub or similar blocking device between the fork-ends when the front wheel is removed from the bike. To verify if the fork is straight, carry out the following alignment check.

Fork Alignment Check

There are several different ways the fork may be bent, each requiring a different test. Proceed as follows:

Tools and equipment
☐ metal straightedge
☐ a perfectly level surface
☐ a perfectly level block, at least 5 cm (2 in) high and about 20 cm (8 in) long
☐ callipers or similar accurate measuring device.

Procedure

1. First check with the straightedge whether the upper portion of the fork blades lies in line with the centerline through the fork shaft (if the fork is still in the bike, line up with the centerline of the head tube). If it's not, either the blades or the fork shaft are bent. If the steering operates smoothly, it will be the fork blades, which can often be corrected (see below); otherwise it will be the fork shaft, which will almost certainly require a new fork.

2. To check whether the fork blades are bent unequally, place the fork on the level surface, resting on the fork-ends, and with the upper portion of the blades on the edge, which must be exactly perpendicular to the fork. If the fork does not rest on all four points, it is misaligned. Note which way it is misaligned by drawing an arrow on the blade that has to be corrected – see below for straightening procedure.

3. To check whether the distance between the blades is correct, check whether the front hub fits snugly, without having to force the fork blades sideways either in or out. If this test shows any misalignment, the last test (point 4) must also be carried out.

4. To check whether the fork is offset laterally, place the fork on the level block (which in turn is on the level sur-

FORK ALIGNMENT CHECK

face) resting on the fork shaft with one blade down. Make sure the blades are exactly vertically above one another, then measure the distance between the lower fork-end and the level surface. Now turn the fork over and do the same check with the other blade down. If the distances are not identical to within 1.5 mm (¹⁄₁₆ in), the fork blades should be cold-set correspondingly. See the description for fork alignment correction below.

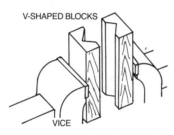

Fork Alignment Correction

As long as the fork is not too severely bent and the steerer tube (fork shaft) is still straight, it will usually be possible to correct misalignment of the fork. This is the same kind of cold setting operation as described for the frame in the preceding chapter. Do it carefully, but not without force. Just clamp the steerer tube in a vice, protecting it with two blocks of wood with V-grooves as shown; place a 24-in long piece of 1½-in diameter tubing over the blade that is to be corrected, as close as possible to the area with the most serious portion of the bend, and force it in the appropriate direction. After bending, carry out the previously described check again, and correct if necessary. Check to make sure there are no sharp irregular bends or cracks before reinstalling the fork. If the fork-ends are not perfectly parallel or are bent, straighten them out by placing them in the vice over their entire length or up to the point of their bend, then force the fork over as required to straighten them.

Front Fork Replacement

To replace a front fork, make sure the new fork has the same blade length, the same rake and the same shaft length. In addition, make sure it has the same kind of threading – French or non-French. The latter condition is most easily established by taking along the head-set locknut when buying the new fork: if it fits on, it is the right threading.

The length of the fork shaft should be selected to correspond to the frame size. Measure the length of the head tube and add to it the so-called stacking height of the head-set, then deduct 1–3 mm (¹⁄₁₆ to ⅛ in). If the fork shaft is too long, it can easily be shortened, but you may have to get the screw thread cut further by a bicycle mechanic to allow installation of the head-set. Finally, it should be considered that not all forks are similarly bent: the amount of rake can vary quite a bit, and will affect the bicycle's steering characteristic considerably. Try to get a new fork that has the same rake as the old one.

The actual replacement work amounts to the same as was described for overhauling the head-set. In addition, it will be necessary to remove the front wheel and anything else attached to the fork. Reinstall all parts again and check whether they are properly aligned and adjusted before using the bike.

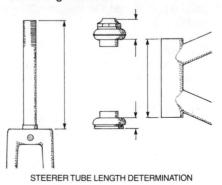

STEERER TUBE LENGTH DETERMINATION

5
Saddle and Seat Post

This will be a very brief chapter indeed: there is not much repair and maintenance work required on the saddle and the seat post (the latter is referred to as seat pin or seat pillar in Britain). We'll look at height and angle adjustment, replacement and care.

Just how high the saddle should be set was already discussed in Chapter 2; here follow the instructions for the actual adjustment work for height, angle and forward position. If the saddle should slip, the seat post may be too small in diameter – get a different size or make a shim as shown below, cut from an aluminum beverage can.

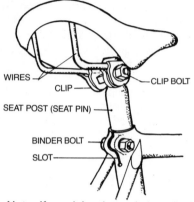

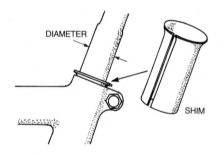

Saddle Height Adjustment
Tools and Equipment
☐ wrench to fit saddle binder bolt (on mountain bikes the presence of a quick-release mechanism makes it possible to adjust the height without tools)

Procedure
1. Loosen the binder bolt, which clamps together the split seat lug, by about one or two turns.
2. Move the saddle up or down in a twisting motion (using the saddle as a lever) until the desired position is reached.
3. Check to make sure the saddle is straight, and tighten the binder bolt.

Note: If a quick-release is installed, merely engage the lever; should the bolt then be too tight or too loose, the thumb-nut at the other end may be loosened or tightened by hand while the lever is in the 'open' position.

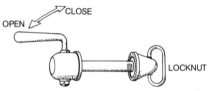

Caution: At least 65 mm (2½ in) of the seat post should remain in the seat tube for adequate hold; it may be necessary to remove the entire seat post, check its length, and mark the maximum protrusion, if the manufacturer has not done so. If the length does not allow the saddle to be placed high enough, either a (special) longer seat post or a different frame size will be required for maximum safety, comfort and efficiency.

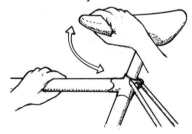

Seat Post Replacement

Follow the same procedures given for seat height adjustment when the seat post must be replaced. Keep the saddle on the seat post for leverage. Make sure to get the right diameter (measured in mm with callipers) and apply a very thin layer of lubricant to the outside of the seat post and the binder bolt, to avoid seizure and corrosion. If the binder bolt cannot be tightened adequately to hold the seat pin, although the right diameter of seat post is used, you may have to file out the gap between the two eyes of the seat lug, using a very thin flat file. To avoid the formation of cracks at the bottom of this cut-out, drill a ⅛-in hole there, if the manufacturer has not done that for you.

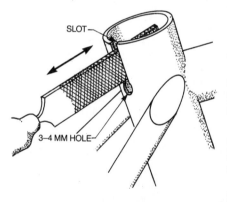

Seat posts come in different types: simple tubular models with a separate saddle clip and micro-adjustable aluminum alloy models. The illustrations show how the most common models look. The big advantage of the adjustable aluminum models is that the angle of the saddle with respect to the horizontal plane can be accurately adjusted, whereas the simple clip only allows quite course adjustments in intervals of about 10 degrees, which may not be satisfactory for long-term comfort.

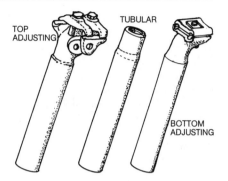

Adjust Saddle Angle and Forward Position

This procedure covers the work with a conventional tubular seat post with separate clip. See the next section for micro-adjustable seat posts.

Tools and Equipment
☐ wrench to fit nut on saddle clip bolt

Procedure
1. Loosen the nut on the clip bolt on one side only, until the serrated outer parts of the clip can be turned with respect to the center parts.
2. Turn the clip until the saddle is under the desired angle, and move it backward or forward until it is in the desired location (see Chapter 2).
3. Holding the saddle firmly in this position, tighten the nut that had been loosened.
Note: If the nut cannot be loosened or tightened adequately, also loosen or tighten the nut on the other side.

Micro-Adjustable Seat Post

To make the same adjustments on a saddle with a micro-adjustable aluminum alloy seat post, the adjustment screws or bolts on top of, or underneath, the adjustment mechanism must be tightened and loosened. On the most common type, loosen both bolts to allow pushing the saddle forward or backward; tighten again when the correct position has been found. To tip the front down, loosen the rear bolt and tighten the one in the front; do the opposite to tilt the front up. To remove the saddle from the seat post, just loosen both bolts until the saddle wires (the metal frame on which the saddle cover is mounted) can be disengaged.

The above description is based on the most typical seat post design. However, there are numerous variations, and it may be necessary to use a little ingenuity to establish how the model in question must be adjusted. A close look under the saddle cover will soon reveal how it is held and how adjustment is achieved.

Saddle Care

There are several distinct types of saddles. Generally considered the most comfortable are those with a self-supporting firm leather cover. These are also the only models that need special care. Don't ever allow the leather cover to get wet, and if it should get wet, don't sit on it until it is

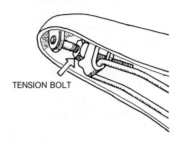

TENSION BOLT

completely dry again, or it will be permanently bent out of shape. Cover the saddle with a plastic bag or a special cover (see Chapter 13 for sewing instructions) whenever you leave the bike outside. From time to time (say once every two months) treat the cover with special preservative (sold in bike stores under the names Proofide or neat's foot oil, although saddle soap will do equally well) from underneath. Take particular care to wrap the saddle in plastic when transporting the bike on a car in the rain. When the tension of the leather cover seems inadequate, it should be tightened with the nut shown in the illustration.

6
The Drive-Train

The bicycle's drive-train consists of the system of components that transmits the rider's effort to the rear wheel: pedals, cranks, bottom bracket, chainwheels, chain and rear sprocket or freewheel assembly. The gearing system – which is considered part of this complex by some authors – will be treated separately in Chapter 7, *Derailleur Gearing* and Chapter 8, *Hub Gearing.*

The Bottom Bracket

The heart of the drive-train is formed by the bottom bracket bearings, to which the cranks and chainwheels are attached. This component is installed in the frame's bottom bracket shell and it is often considered part of a larger sub-assembly called the crank-set: bottom bracket with cranks and chainwheels. Though the bottom bracket unit may be bought and replaced separately, it must be selected to match the other components of the crank-set. There are several different types, which are not mutually interchangeable – at least not without also replacing other components of the crank-set.

The illustrations with the individual instructions show the different types, and should help you in distinguishing the type installed on the bike in question. Typical bottom bracket problems are evidenced by irregular pedaling motion, high resistance when pedaling, or perceptible 'play' in the bearings. By way of regular maintenance, I recommend checking and adjusting on a regular basis once a month and overhauling once or twice a year. Adjustments can be carried out with the cranks still on the bike; to overhaul or lubricate, the cranks must be removed – descriptions of that work will be given in subsequent sections of this chapter.

Adjust BSA Bottom Bracket

This is the most common type of bottom bracket on quality bicycles. The bearing cups are screwed into the bottom bracket shell – the fixed RH cup all the way, the adjustable LH cup only partway and then countered with a lockring. Adjusting amounts to screwing the adjustable cup further in or out and then locking in the correct position. If the problem cannot be alleviated this way, the bearing must be overhauled.

Tools and equipment
☐ either: special lockring wrench and pin wrench for the make and model of bottom bracket in question, or: hammer and drift or pin

Procedure
1. Loosen the lockring on the left hand side of the bottom bracket by turning to the left from the cut-outs in the lockring.
2. Tighten or loosen the adjustable cup.
3. Holding the cup to prevent it from turning with the lockring, tighten the lockring again.
4. Check to make sure the bearing is properly adjusted now, and make any corrections that may be required.
Note: To establish play (i.e. looseness) in the bearing, it is best to check with the cranks installed; to make sure

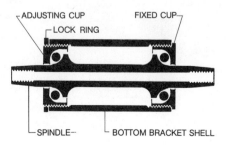

ADJUSTING CUP   FIXED CUP
LOCK RING
SPINDLE   BOTTOM BRACKET SHELL

the bearing runs smoothly and freely, it is best to remove both cranks and the chainwheels, so that the axle can be easily turned with the fingers of the hand.

Note: It is preferable to use special bottom bracket tools for these two procedures (adjusting and overhauling). It is, nevertheless, possible to do the entire job with the provisional tools listed above, providing you work very carefully. In that case, the lockring can be loosened or tightened with a drift or a *blunt* cold chisel by placing it in one of the notches and tapping it with a hammer in the appropriate direction. Similarly, the adjustable cup can be screwed in or out by placing a drift in one of the recesses and carefully tapping it in the appropriate direction with a hammer.

Overhaul BSA Bottom Bracket

Before commencing this work, the cranks must be removed from the bottom bracket spindle; for instructions see the appropriate section of this chapter.

Tools and equipment
☐ either: special lockring wrench and pin wrench for the make and model of bottom bracket in question, or: hammer and drift or pin
☐ rags
☐ bearing grease
☐ if fixed cup (RH side) must be removed: fitting wrench or a metalworking vice

Disassembly procedure

1. Remove the lockring on the LH side by unscrewing to the left.

2. Remove the adjustable cup by unscrewing to the left; remove the bearing balls (usually held in a retainer).

3. Pull out the bottom bracket spindle and remove the bearing balls on the chain side.

4. Clean and inspect all parts. Replace any part that is pitted, grooved or corroded. I suggest always replacing the bearing balls.

5. If the RH (fixed) cup is also to be replaced, remove it by unscrewing it. Note that it may have either RH screw thread (if it is threaded to either BCI, i.e. British, or Swiss standards) or LH screw thread (if it is threaded to either French or Italian standards).

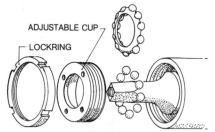

Note: When replacing parts, make absolutely sure to get the right type and (especially the spindle) the right size, by taking the spindle and the bearing cups as well as the lockring to the store. Try to screw the new cup in the old lockring, comparing the length and shape of the spindle, and check to establish whether both the new and the old fixed cups have either LH or

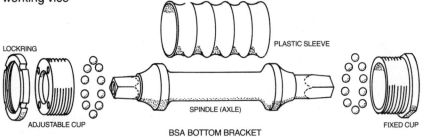

BSA BOTTOM BRACKET

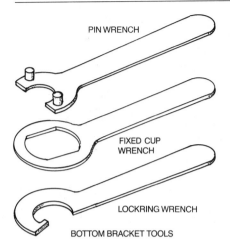

PIN WRENCH

FIXED CUP
WRENCH

LOCKRING WRENCH

BOTTOM BRACKET TOOLS

8. Check and adjust again after the cranks have been installed, since play in the bearings is easier to detect over the leverage of the cranks.

Note: If you should misalign the threads when trying to reinstall the cups, get the thread re-cut by a bike mechanic; alternatively, install a cartridge bearing unit.

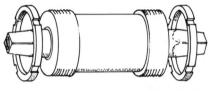

CARTRIDGE BEARING (SEALED) BOTTOM BRACKET

RH threading (see Chapter 2). Clean all parts and lubricate lightly before assembling.

Assembly procedure
1. Install the fixed cup on the RH side; screw up firmly to the left if it has LH thread, to the right if it has RH thread.
2. Fill both bearing cups with bearing grease, and place the balls inside. If the balls are not held in a retainer, use one ball less than the absolute maximum number that would seem to fit in.
3. Put the spindle in with the longer end first (so it will protrude from the RH or fixed cup).
4. Place a plastic sleeve over the spindle; this will help keep out dirt, water and rust that might otherwise enter through the seat tube or (on some bikes) through cut-outs in the bottom bracket shell.
5. Install the LH (adjustable) cup just far enough to allow the spindle to turn freely without play.
6. Install the lockring, holding the adjustable cup in place.
7. Check for smooth operation without play, and make any adjustments that may be required.

Sealed Bearing Units
Pre-assembled bottom bracket units with sealed cartridge bearings are becoming increasingly popular, especially on mountain bikes. Some of these are relatively easy to remove with the aid of screwed retainer rings, similar to the cups and lockring on the conventional BSA type bottom bracket bearings. Other models are pushed into the bottom bracket shell. A look at the bottom bracket will soon reveal whether the unit may be easily removed or not. Special tools are available for most models, and it is usually simpler to replace the entire unit than it is to overhaul the individual bearings. See a bike mechanic for any real problems.

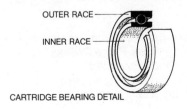

OUTER RACE

INNER RACE

CARTRIDGE BEARING DETAIL

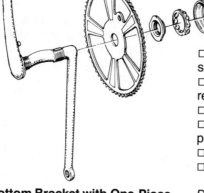

□ wrench to fit cone on chainwheel side
□ large screwdriver (if cups must be replaced)
□ hammer (if cups must be replaced)
□ block of wood (if cups must be re-placed)
□ rag
□ bearing grease

Bottom Bracket with One-Piece Cranks

One-piece cranks are traditionally popular on cheaper American bicycles. The illustration shows how they are installed. Here the bearing cups are pushed into the ends of the bottom bracket shell, and adjustable cones are screwed on the spindle, which forms one integral part with the two cranks. To adjust, proceed as follows:

Tools and equipment
□ medium size screwdriver
□ wrench to fit locknut on LH side

Adjusting procedure
1. Loosen the locknut on the LH side by turning it to the right (it has LH thread) while holding the crank.
2. Lift the lock washer and turn the underlying cone with the screwdriver to the right to loosen, or to the left to tighten, the bearing.
3. Hold the cone in place while tightening the locknut to the left.

Overhaul Bottom Bracket with One-Piece Cranks

Tools and equipment
□ medium size screwdriver
□ wrench to fit locknut

Disassembly procedure
1. Remove the LH pedal (see elsewhere in this chapter)
2. Unscrew LH locknut to the right (LH screw thread) and remove locknut and lock washer.
3. Unscrew the adjustable (LH) cone, and remove the cone and the bearing retainer.
4. Wriggle the chainwheel out free from the chain and pull the entire Z-shaped crank unit out towards the RH (chain) side of the bike.
5. Remove the bearing retainer of the RH side bearing.
6. Inspect all parts; replace the bearing ball retainers and any parts that are grooved, pitted or corroded.

Note: The RH cone can be removed by simply unscrewing it, which will also loosen the chainwheel. The bearing cups can be removed by hammering them out, using the large

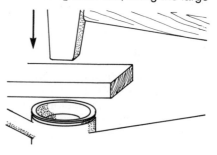

screwdriver. Follow the illustration for reinstallation; the cups must be driven home until they are firmly seated.

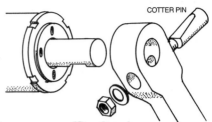

Assembly procedure

1. Start reassembling after cleaning and lubricating all parts; put bearing grease in both cups, then screw the fixed cone back up over the chainwheel on the RH crank.

2. Install the bearing ball retainer in the RH cup, then insert the crank unit from the RH side.

3. Install the LH bearing retainer in the grease-packed LH cup; screw the adjustable cone on to the left (LH thread), followed by the keyed lock washer and the locknut. Adjust for optimal operation: running smoothly without play.

4. Install the pedal and the chain.

The Cranks

Apart from the integral one-piece crank construction, there are two different methods of joining cranks to the bottom bracket spindle: cottered and cotterless. The cotterless system is used more and more these days, and usually is associated with aluminum

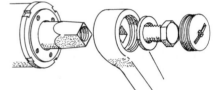

Thompson Bottom Bracket

Chances are you'll never see one of these. It is the standard on cheap northern European (especially German) bicycles and as such sometimes found in Britain, but very rarely on the American continent. The illustration shows how it's put together. Assembly and disassembly is started from the LH side. The locknut has LH thread and must be loosened (to the right) before adjusting. Adjusting (or removing and installing) the adjustable cone is done by turning the keyed dustcap, which has teeth that engage in slots in the adjustable cone. All very clever and very simple once you know the trick. The bearing cups are press-fit into the bottom bracket shell – removal and installation as for one-piece cranks.

cranks. The spindle has square tapered ends and the cranks have corresponding holes and a big recess from the other side. A bolt or nut in the recess keeps the crank on the spindle – tighten this bolt or nut from time to time to avoid it getting loose, and certainly tighten it whenever the crank seems loose, as evidenced by play or disturbing noises in the cranks. The other system relies on a wedge-shaped cotter pin with a nut at the end that is seated in a groove in the spindle and a hole in the crank. Also this thing has to be tightened from time to time. A bent crank results in an awkward pedalling motion and can be straightened at a bike shop with a special tool: it's not advisable to try to do this work yourself.

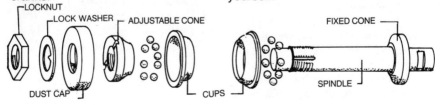

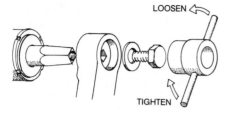

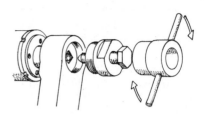

LOOSEN

TIGHTEN

Tighten Cotterless Crank
Tools and equipment
☐ wrench-part of special crank tool (these tools come in at least two sizes: one size to fit assemblies with 15 mm bolts and one to fit 14 mm bolts – people who sell these tools in bike stores should know which type fits your make and model of crank-set)

Procedure
1. Remove the dust cap, which is screwed into the recess of the crank.
2. Tighten the crank bolt or nut with the special wrench, countering from the crank (an excellent way is to stop the crank from turning by blocking it against the frame with a stick or tube, inserted through the frame and behind the crank).
3. Reinstall the dust cap.

Remove and Install Cotterless Crank
Tools and equipment
☐ special crank extractor tool to fit the make and model of the crank
☐ rag
☐ vaseline or special anti-seize lubricant

Removal procedure
1. Remove dust cap.
2. Remove crank bolt or nut.
3. Remove washer.
4. Retract the puller part of the crank extractor tool and screw it into the recess in the crank by at least four turns, then tighten the inner part of the tool to push the crank off the spindle. Remove the tool from the crank.

Installation procedure
1. Clean all mating surfaces and screw threads; inspect for cracks (don't install a cracked crank) and apply a light layer of vaseline or special anti-seize lubricant to the mating surfaces of the spindle and the crank hole.
2. Place the crank on the spindle (the crank with the chainwheel attachment on the right – longer spindle end), the cranks 180° off-set.
3. Install the washer and the bolt or the nut and tighten it, using the wrench part of the crank extractor tool.
4. Install the dust cap.
Note: Retighten after riding about 25 miles (40 km), especially if this is a new crank, since the surfaces deform slightly as they are seated. If the crank (on the chainwheel side) is too close to the frame, so the chainwheel rubs against the chain stay, the square hole in the crank is slightly too big; you may correct this by installing an improvised thin aluminum shim as illustrated, cut from an aluminum beverage can. Again, retightening will be required at least once during the first 25 miles of use.

IMPROVISED SHIM

One-Key Release

Some cotterless crank-sets are equipped with a one-key release system, which can be operated with a single Allen key without the need for a special extractor. Here the crank attachment bolt is in the form of an Allen bolt; the place of the dustcap is taken by a stronger screwed insert, installed with a special pin wrench and held in place with locking adhesive. When the bolt, which is accessible through a hole in this insert, is unscrewed, its head soon hits the inside of the insert and forces the crank off the axle as it is unscrewed further.

Installation is just as simple: place the crank on the axle, making sure to line up the screwed end of the bolt with the screwed hole in the axle; then tighten the bolt. If the insert gives the slightest hint of coming loose, take it out, clean the screw thread, and cement it in with anaerobic locking adhesive. Once the insert were lost, you would find it impossible to remove the crank.

ONE-KEY RELEASE

Remove and Install Cottered Crank

Tools and Equipment
☐ wrench to fit nut on cotter pin
☐ hammer
☐ something solid to support crank

Removal procedure
1. Unscrew nut on cotter pin until the end of the cotter pin is about 1.5 mm. (1/16 in) below the top of the nut, or by at least two full turns, whichever is more.
2. Supporting the crank with something solid, hammer down the nut until it touches the crank.

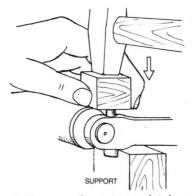

SUPPORT

3. Unscrew the nut completely and push or hammer the cotter pin out; remove the crank.

Installation procedure
1. Place the crank on the spindle. Note that the hole in the crank must be lined up with the groove in the spindle, and that the crank with the chainwheel or the attachment for the chainwheel is on the RH side (chain side) of the bike.
2. Place the cotter pin through the crank from the bigger hole (assuming one of the holes is bigger, which can easily be verified by trying to put the cotter pin in from both sides). The flat side of the cotter pin must be aligned with the groove in the spindle.
3. Supporting the crank with something solid, hammer the cotton pin in until enough screw thread protrudes to install the washer and the nut, then tighten the nut fully; hammer down and tighten again.

Note: If the cotter pin is damaged or if the thread is worn so much that

the nut feels loose, it should be replaced by one of the same diameter
(several different diameters are in use)
although, by way of temporary repair,
installing a second nut (locknut) may
do the trick. Filing the flat face down
until it is smooth will be sufficient if the
cotter pin is not too seriously deform-
ed. Tighten again after about 25 miles
of use. If for some reason the crank
must be replaced, make sure to get
one for the same spindle diameter
and the same pedal thread size (see
instructions for pedal replacement
elsewhere in this chapter).

The Chainwheels

One or more chainwheels are attached to the RH crank. On cheap simple
bikes one of these may be permanently attached, but generally they
are interchangeable. Only the latter
case is of interest for maintenance
instructions, since for a permanently
attached chainwheel the entire unit of
crank and chainwheel must be replaced in case of wear or damage.

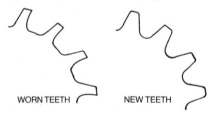

WORN TEETH   NEW TEETH

It may be necessary to replace the
chainwheels if they are badly worn.
Worn chainwheels have teeth that
take on the form shown in the illustration. Sometimes chainwheels are replaced because the owner isn't satis-
fied with the range of gearing that is
possible with the particular chainwheel size installed on the bike. To
get a lower range of gears, a smaller
chainwheel must be selected – just
make sure the other components of
the gearing system, especially the
rear derailleur, can handle the particular combination that results, and

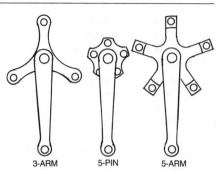

3-ARM   5-PIN   5-ARM

that the chain length is changed to
suit. Finally, the teeth or the chainwheel body may be bent or damaged:
in this case, correction by bending or
hammering may be possible, but if it
isn't, it must be replaced.

Although many manufacturers
make similar looking chainwheels, it
will still be necessary to be careful
when replacing a chainwheel, since
there are quite a number of different
attachment details particular to specific makes and models. The illustration
shows a number of different configurations that may be used. In addition,
the diameter of the bolt circle can vary
quite a bit. Take the old RH crank and
any other parts to which the chainwheel in question will be attached
(e.g. the big chainwheel, if you are replacing the smaller one and if it is attached to it, instead of to the crank)
and the attachment bolts (because
these too may have different dimensions) to the shop with you when buying the new chainwheel.

When replacing the chainwheel,
the RH crank may be removed from
the bike (see the appropriate description elsewhere in this chapter). On a
one-piece crank the entire crankset
must be removed, after which you unscrew the RH bearing cone to get at
the chainwheel. When reinstalling,
fit the hole in the chainwheel over the
peg on the crank. On other models, a
close look at the attachments will soon
enough reveal just what has to be

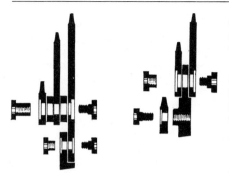

done to remove the chainwheels; just take care to reinstall them the right way round (watch for the recessed side of the attachment holes) and to seat the screws and the spacers properly. Tighten the attachment screws firmly and retighten after some 25 miles of use.

Straighten Chainwheels

Chainwheels or individual teeth may get bent, especially during transportation of the bicycle, or as the result of a crash. Typical symptoms are high and irregular resistance while pedalling, and scraping of the chain or the chainwheel, as well as frequent derailing of the chain. Usually the chainwheel can be kept on the bike while it is being straightened. Individual teeth may be bent back into shape by holding them with a crescent wrench and twisting it in the appropriate direction, as shown in the illustration. Replace the chainwheel if during straightening individual teeth break or show serious cracks.

A bent chainwheel is usually noticed when the chain comes off the

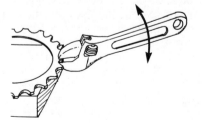

chainwheel frequently, or when intermittent scraping of the chain against the frame or the front derailleur occurs. Use a big wrench, a mallet or a combination of these to straighten the chainwheel. To verify whether it is indeed straight, observe the distance between the chainwheel and the RH rear stay as you slowly rotate the cranks.

The Chain

The bicycle's chain is a very clever and effective transmission element, which deserves a lot more care than it usually gets. It should be cleaned and lubricated frequently to avoid excessive wear and inefficient operation. Depending on the kind of use and maintenance it receives, it should be replaced after anything from 2000 to 5000 miles when it can be lifted off the chainwheel by ⅛ in (3 mm).

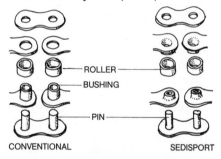

CONVENTIONAL   SEDISPORT

The illustration shows the two construction methods for the chain. The least susceptible to wear appears to be the one illustrated on the right, as made under the trade name Sedisport. On the other extreme are models with 'bulging' inner link plates, such as the Shimano Uniglide chain, which not only wear, but actually stretch under the effect of high pedalling forces. This latter type should only be used by riders who always ride in low gears and never pedal with much

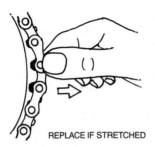

REPLACE IF STRETCHED

force. Special compact freewheel assemblies with 6 or 7 sprockets generally require the use of special chains – ask in the bike store.

In addition to these two different designs, there are two sizes commonly in use. Both types have the same link length, measured as the distance between two consecutive connecting pins at ½ in, but differ in width. The width is measured between the inside link plates, and is either ⅛ in (for track racing bicycles, three-speeds and utility bikes with coaster brakes) or ³⁄₃₂ in for all derailleur bikes. The wider chains used for three-speeds and utility bikes usually are connected in one place with a special removable link, called chain lock or master link, as illustrated; it must be installed in the orientation shown, so it does not work itself loose while cycling.

Other chains are usually joined by pushing the pin of the last link into the bushing of the first link, although special (narrow) chain locks are available under the trade name Super Link. If you use a chain lock, I suggest you mark it e.g. with bright orange paint, so you can find it amongst the more than 100 links on the bicycle chain

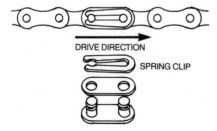

DRIVE DIRECTION

SPRING CLIP

when the chain must be removed. Since the use of the chain lock is simple enough, the instructions that follow will be restricted to handling the chain without such chain lock.

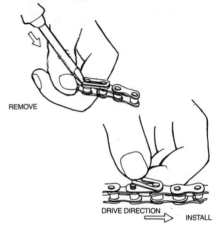

REMOVE

DRIVE DIRECTION
INSTALL

Chain Maintenance
Tools and equipment
☐ chain rivet extractor tool
☐ rag
☐ kerosene (British: paraffin oil)
☐ chain lubricant – preferably special lubricant with molybdenum disulfide ('moly'), although mineral motor oil, synthetic oil and, in dry and dusty regions, paraffin wax (candle wax) can be used successfully

Removal procedure
1. Retract the chain extractor fully, then place it on one of the chain link pins as shown, and turn it in until the pin of the tool touches the chain link pin firmly.
2. Screw in the handle until the pin protrudes on the other side just far enough to undo the link when the tool has been withdrawn and removed.
Note: It's best to practice this on an old piece of chain first, so you learn to judge just how far you should push the pin out. If you push it too far, reinstallation will be very tricky, since the two end links will not stay in place. If the

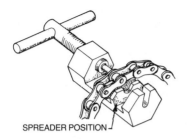

SPREADER POSITION

object is to shorten the chain, on the other hand, push the pin out all the way at one end of the section that will be removed.

Cleaning and lubrication procedure

1. Wash out the chain in kerosene or other solvent to which some mineral oil should be added (about one part in ten), to inhibit the formation of rust. Use a small bottle brush to clean between the links.

2. Rinse out in clean solvent (to obtain that, just let the stuff you used before stand about 10 minutes, then carefully pour it into another container, taking care not disturb the settled dirt at the bottom, which you will discard).

3. Allow the chain to drip about 10 minutes, then wipe it with a rag and immediately lubricate with the chosen lubricant. Synthetic oil is available in spray cans, as are some special chain lubricants. Paraffin wax and some types of special chain lubricant (e.g. Castrol Motorcycle Chain Lube as

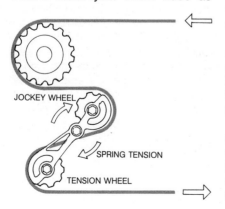

JOCKEY WHEEL

SPRING TENSION

TENSION WHEEL

available in Britain, namely in a big flat can) are heated in boiling hot water to melt them, then the chain is submerged in the liquid lubricant, allowed to soak it up for about five minutes and removed again using pliers, after which it is allowed to drip and cool off; finally the outside is wiped clean. If spray can lubricant is used, spray it on the *inside* of the chain.

Installation procedure

1. Before installing, establish whether the chain has the right length (it must just fit around the biggest sprocket and the biggest chainwheel, while leaving just a little movement in the derailleur); if necessary, remove or add the appropriate even number of links. Keep any links removed, in case you later have to add or replace chain links.

2. Place the chain around the small chainwheel and the smallest sprocket, with the pin that has been pushed out facing the outside (RH side) of the bike.

3. Wriggle the two end links together and use the chain rivet extractor to push the link pin back into the link, making sure the hole in the opposite outer link plate is aligned with the pin (if it isn't, the link plate will get bent – in that case you must replace the link with a new one).

4. Check and, if necessary, correct the protrusion of the link pin, which must be the same on both sides.

5. Make sure the links at this connection are free to move relative to one another – twist these links a little to loosen them up if necessary, or use the tool to spread the link in the spreader slot, turning it in just slightly.

Note: Especially on bikes without a derailleur, the position of the rear wheel in the rear drop-outs may have to be varied to fine-tune the length of the chain: without a derailleur, it should be just long enough to allow

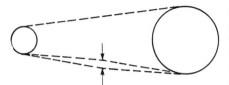

a movement of about ¾ in up and down.

Chain Line

For the most efficient transmission of power, the chain should lie in the same plane as the front chainwheel and the rear sprocket with which it is engaged. On bicycles with derailleur gearing this situation can at best be approached remotely for most gearing combinations. To do at least that, the chain line should be so that the center of the assembly of all sprockets lies in the same plane as the center of the chainwheel combination. In practical terms that means that for a ten-speed the middle sprocket should be lined up with a point just halfway between the two chainwheels; for a fifteen-speed the middle sprocket is lined up with the middle chainwheel. If a freewheel with six sprockets is used, the center of this combination will be halfway between the third and the fourth sprocket.

On a well designed and assembled bicycle the chain line will be correct; however, abuse, part replacement or maladjustment can all cause the chain line to get out of wack. Correcting the chain line is one of the trickiest jobs in bicycle maintenance and defies systematic instruction techniques, especially in those cases where the problem existed from the start, as is often the case with less carefully designed and assembled bicycles. Check by careful observation from behind, and determine whether the judicious use of spacers on either the rear wheel (on the axle or between hub and freewheel) or the crank-set (e.g. the home-made shim described in the section on crank installation elsewhere in this chapter) will do the trick. If not only the chain line, but also the wheels themselves are misaligned in the same direction, the two problems can sometimes be simultaneously solved with cold-setting (bending) the frame, as described in Chapter 3, *The Frame*. But keep in mind that this work involves three variables: frame, transmission and wheel: consider all the possible effects before attempting such a drastic measure, and make any further corrections to offset any problems caused by it.

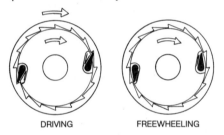

DRIVING   FREEWHEELING

The Freewheel

With the exception of directly driven machines with a so-called fixed wheel, such as track racing bikes, all modern bicycles have a freewheel mechanism built into or installed on the rear wheel hub. On virtually all derailleur bicycles and single-speed bikes with rim brakes (the latter rare enough in the USA, but not unknown elsewhere), the freewheel forms a separate unit to which the sprocket is attached, and which itself is screwed onto the rear wheel hub. Other bikes have a rear hub

with integral freewheel mechanism; these will be discussed whenever the type of equipment with which they are combined is considered (e.g. hub gearing in Chapter 8 and coaster brakes in Chapter 10). Here I shall concentrate on the separate freewheel mechanism installed on most bicycles in use today.

There are literally dozens of different models, and quite a few different manufacturers of freewheels. Though almost all are mutually interchangeable as a complete unit, it is rarely possible to install parts of one model on another: sprockets that fit the one, will generally not fit another. There are several other differences between the various types. The screw threading with which they are attached to the hub may differ, there being French and Italian standards that are not mutually interchangeable, and an English standard that is so close to the Italian standard as to allow interchangeability with it without serious damage.

There are also some freewheel types that are so different from all others as to restrict their use to one particular matching hub – Maillard's Helico-Matic and Shimano's Cassette Freehub being the most popular examples in this category. Finally, many freewheel bodies will accept only a certain number of sprockets in certain sizes: some take five, others may take six or seven sprockets; some may be used with wide-range gearing (i.e. big differences in sprocket sizes), whereas other models will only accept sprockets for narrow range (i.e. racing) gearing. The number of different peculiarities to keep in mind is so great that I cannot list them all here: ask at the bike shop to find out what will suit your purpose and what won't.

Freewheel maintenance includes cleaning, lubrication, removal and the replacement of individual sprockets. When I first got involved with bike maintenance, the latter was no big

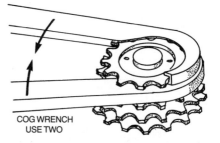

COG WRENCH
USE TWO

problem: all freewheels at that time seemed to be assembled quite similarly. With the entry of the Japanese manufacturers in the late 'sixties, things haven't got any simpler: today sprockets are still interchangeable, but you must find out for each individual type just how which particular sprocket is held on. Usually the smallest sprocket is the one that wears out fastest (as evidenced by a new chain climbing up on the teeth and then 'jumping'). This particular sprocket is nearly always screwed directly onto the freewheel body or the underlying next bigger sprocket with RH thread. Use a special freewheel cog wrench to undo this sprocket, countering on the next sprocket with a second wrench. To install, thread the sprocket on by hand, then tighten with the two wrenches.

Freewheel Removal and Installation

This work is often required to get access to the hub for spoke replacement. Otherwise it only needs to be done to replace the entire freewheel, because maintenance, lubrication and the most important sprocket replacements can all be carried out with the freewheel mounted on the hub of the rear wheel. Take the wheel out of the bike first.

Tools and equipment
☐ freewheel extractor tool for the make and model of freewheel in question
☐ wrench to fit the freewheel extractor (alternately: metal-working vice)

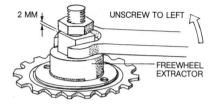

☐ rag
☐ lubricant (e.g. acid-free vaseline or special anti-seize lubricant)

Removal procedure

1. Place the freewheel extractor tool in the splines or notches of the free-wheel, over the hub bearing locknut (if it fits there – if not, remove the lock-nut first), and hold it in place with the quick-release lever or the axle nut, allowing about 1.5 mm ($^1/_{16}$ in) of free-dom in the axial direction.

2. Hold the wheel very firmly (e.g. with the tire compressed between your belly and the walls of the room where they meet in a corner) and turn the extractor one full turn to the left with the wrench. Alternately, the ex-tractor may be held in the vice while you turn the wheel counterclockwise by one turn.

3. Loosen the axle nut or quick-release nut one full turn and continue, each time loosening the nut enough to give you axial freedom for one more turn, until the freewheel comes off the hub.

Installation procedure

1. Before installing, clean the screw thread of freewheel body and hub, then apply vaseline or anti-seize lubri-cant to these surfaces. When install-ing a new freewheel, make sure it has the same kind of screw thread as the hub (French, Italian, special). You may also wish to install a so-called spoke protector between the hub flange and the freewheel body; this is a round plate that stops the derailleur and the chain from getting caught in the spokes if the derailleur is improperly

adjusted and pushes the chain too far – beyond the biggest sprocket.

2. Carefully match the screw thread of the freewheel with that of the hub and screw it on by hand. Final tighten-ing will take place 'automatically' as soon as you start pedalling.

3. After cycling a short distance – enough to tighten the freewheel on the hub – readjust the rear derailleur so it reaches all gears (see Chapter 7, *Derailleur Gearing*).

Freewheel Lubrication

Since for most freewheels minor parts are not available for replacement, I shall not give complete overhauling instructions. What will be covered here deals with the most frequent free-wheel problems: rough running and wobbling. If the problem is rough rota-tion, sometimes aggravated by occa-sional 'refusal' to freewheel (i.e. the freewheel and the rest of the drive-train continue to turn with the rear wheel, although the rider intends to keep the pedals still), lubrication may offer a simple cure.

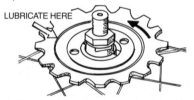

1. Place the wheel on its side, the freewheel facing up (the rear wheel may be kept in the bike), and a con-tainer, like a sizable old tin can, under the hub to catch the excess lubricant.

2. Pour a thin-flowing lubricant into the gap shown in the illustration be-tween the stationary and the rotating part of the mechanism, as the rear wheel is turned back. This acts both to flush out dirt and to lubricate: just keep pouring in the oil until it comes out clean the other side.

3. Allow to drip until no more oil is seeping through; wipe off excess oil.

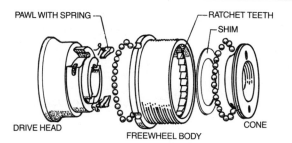

PAWL WITH SPRING — RATCHET TEETH — SHIM

DRIVE HEAD   FREEWHEEL BODY   CONE

Minor Freewheel Overhaul

Do this work to eliminate the wobbling effect of an obviously loose freewheel mechanism. In addition, it may be worthwhile in other cases of freewheel trouble, since you may solve the problem without having to replace the freewheel. First remove the rear wheel from the bike, but leave the freewheel on the hub. Clean the outside of the freewheel (also between the sprockets) before commencing.

Tools and equipment
☐ special pin wrench or a drift and a hammer
☐ rag
☐ bearing grease
☐ 12–15 in twine

UNSCREW TO RIGHT

Procedure
1. Using hammer and drift (or special fitting pin wrench) unscrew the part shown in the illustration; this is actually the freewheel bearing cone and has LH screw thread: unscrew it by turning to the right.
2. Remove the shim (or one of several shims) that is installed under the cone. This will close up the gap between the two bearing races and will usually solve the wobbling.

Note: If you had another problem, proceed disassembling the mechanism to establish whether it can be corrected. Embed the bearing balls in a generous layer of bearing grease. The illustration shows how to hold the mechanism together so it can be reinserted in the freewheel housing.

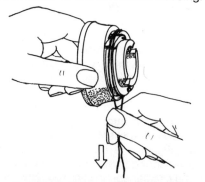

3. Reinstall the freewheel bearing cone by screwing to the left, tightening firmly; then check whether it is operating smoothly now. If necessary, remove an other shim or replace it with one of an other thickness.

Fixed Wheel Sprocket

A track racing bike uses a fixed wheel. This is also possible to use on a bike ridden on the road – it is considered an excellent way to develop a smooth pedalling style – as long as you don't try it in hilly terrain, and providing you choose a low enough gear ratio to allow pedalling with relative ease.

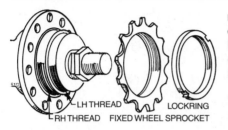

LH THREAD   LOCKRING
RH THREAD   FIXED WHEEL SPROCKET

The illustration shows how the fixed sprocket is installed on the cleaned and lubricated threading of the track hub: it is screwed on, then locked in place with a lockring that's installed on the portion of the hub that has LH screw thread. Both must be tightened very securely, and retightened after some use. The lockring may be removed (turning to the right: LH thread) with a special wrench or with a hammer and drift; use a normal sprocket puller to unscrew the sprocket from the hub.

Sprocket on Hub with Integral Freewheel Mechanism

This description applies to coaster brakes, gear hubs and other forms of hub brakes which have a freewheel mechanism built into the hub. Here the rear sprocket is generally held on splines on the hub's freewheel mechanism and kept in place by means of a circular spring clip. You may wish to replace the sprocket to achieve a different gearing (choose a smaller sprocket to make all gears higher, a bigger sprocket to get lower gears). You may then have to adjust the chain length as well. This work may also be

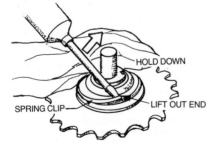

HOLD DOWN
SPRING CLIP   LIFT OUT END

required to turn a (dished) sprocket over to make changes to the chain line or to replace a badly worn sprocket. Remove the wheel from the bike before commencing.

Tools and equipment
☐ narrow screwdriver
☐ rag

Procedure
1. Place the rear wheel flat down in front of you with the sprocket facing up.
2. Hold one end of the spring clip down with the rag, while prying out the other end with the screwdriver; then gradually work the entire clip out, using the rag to prevent its catapulting out.
3. Before reinstalling, clean all parts. Place the sprocket on the hub, oriented the appropriate way if it is a dished model; then place one end of the spring clip in the groove and gradually work the rest in, keeping it down with the rag.

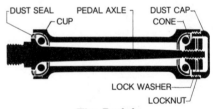

DUST SEAL   PEDAL AXLE   DUST CAP
CUP   CONE
LOCK WASHER
LOCKNUT

The Pedals

Pedals get quite a beating, being subjected to significant forces on asymetrically loaded bearings, which are often not very well sealed against dirt and moisture. Adjust or overhaul the pedals when they are not running smoothly or when they have developed perceptible play in the bearings. If an irregular pedalling motion is noticed, the pedal axle may be bent – you may have to replace the entire pedal in that case, since such spare parts are not available for most makes.

The illustration shows a cross section through a typical pedal with adjustable bearings. There are also cheap, inferior non-adjustable models and – on the other end of the price scale – expensive pedals with sealed cartridge bearings. The latter are not adjustable either, but they will run very smoothly without maintenance for a long time. When they do malfunction, take them to a bike shop to have the cartridge bearings replaced, since that requires special tools. All other bearings can be adjusted or overhauled quite easily.

Pedal Bearing Adjustment

You may leave the pedal on the crank for this work.

Tools and equipment
☐ wrench to remove dust cap
☐ open-ended wrench to fit locknut
☐ small screwdriver (or whatever else will allow adjusting the cone)

Procedure
1. Remove the dust cap.
2. Loosen the locknut by at least one full turn.
3. Lift lock washer and loosen or tighten the adjusting cone.
4. Tighten the locknut again, making sure the cone does not turn with it. If the lock washer's internal prong is worn off, so the washer turns with the locknut, it must be replaced, since it would not allow tightening the locknut without also affecting the cone adjustment.
5. Check the adjustment and make any corrections that may be necessary to obtain smooth running without noticeable bearing play. Proceed to a complete overhaul (or replace the en-

tire pedal) if the adjustment process does not lead to the desired result.
6. Install the dust cap.

Pedal Overhaul

Also this work can be done with the pedal attached to the bike.

Tools and equipment
☐ wrench for dust cap
☐ wrench to fit locknut
☐ small screwdriver (or whatever else will allow adjusting the cone)
☐ bearing grease
☐ rag

Disassembly procedure
1. Remove dust cap.
2. Remove locknut.
3. Remove lock washer.
4. Remove adjustable cone, catching the bearing balls in the rag.
5. Pull the pedal housing off the axle, catching the bearing balls at the other end.
Note: Inspect all parts and replace the bearing balls, as well as anything that is obviously bent, pitted, grooved or corroded. Replace the lock washer if the internal projection is worn off. Clean all bearing parts.

Assembly procedure
1. Fill the bearing cups at both ends of the pedal housing with bearing grease, and install the bearing balls: to assure they don't fit too tightly, use one less than the absolute maximum number that would seem to fit in.
2. Place the pedal housing over the spindle, taking care not to lose any of the bearing balls.
3. Screw the adjustable bearing cone into place, followed by the keyed lock washer and the locknut.
4. Check the adjustment of the bearing, and readjust if necessary.
5. Install the dust cap.

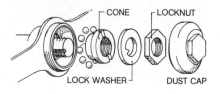

CONE   LOCKNUT
LOCK WASHER   DUST CAP

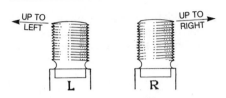

L   R

UP TO LEFT ◄

UP TO RIGHT ►

Remove and Install Pedal

Note that there are actually three different threading standards for pedals: French, British (which is the same as Italian) and American (used on bikes with one-piece cranks). Make sure to get the right type. Whatever the type, the RH pedal has RH thread, the LH pedal LH thread.

Tools and equipment
☐ special pedal wrench or any other wrench that fits either the flats on the spindle or (on some pedals) a hexagonal recess in the end of the spindle's screwed stub, reached from the back of the crank when the pedal is installed
☐ vaseline or anti-seize lubricant
☐ rag

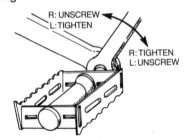

R: UNSCREW
L: TIGHTEN

R: TIGHTEN
L: UNSCREW

Removal procedure
1. For the RH pedal (i.e. on the chain side), unscrew by turning the pedal spindle counterclockwise, restraining the crank.
2. For the LH pedal, turn clockwise in the same manner.

Installation procedure
1. Clean the crank and the threaded stub on the pedal spindle, then smear vaseline or anti-seize lubricant on the mating surfaces lightly.

2. For the RH pedal, screw on by turning clockwise.
3. For the LH pedal, screw on by turning counterclockwise.

Pedal Thread Inserts

When the screw thread in the soft aluminum crank of a cotterless crankset is stripped to the point where the pedal does not fit tightly, it is possible to install a special thread insert. This is a spring-steel coil in the exact shape of the pedal thread. Get it installed at the bike shop, since the old hole in the crank must be drilled out to the exact dimension prescribed by the manufacturer. This same method may be used to convert one type of pedal thread to the other.

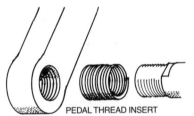

PEDAL THREAD INSERT

Toeclip Installation

This job does not warrant a step-by-step instruction. Follow the illustration for the routing of the toe-strap, so that it does not slip through the pedal too lightly. Make sure to get the toeclip size that matches your shoe size (small up to size 6½, medium up to size 8, large for bigger feet). If necessary, bend the toeclip to suit your shoe size and pedal position, leaving about 1/16 to 1/8 in between the tip of the shoe and the inside of the toeclip.

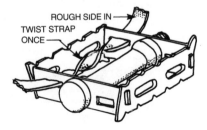

ROUGH SIDE IN ►
TWIST STRAP ONCE

Tandem Drive-Train

There are several different configurations used to connect the two crank-sets and the rear wheel on a tandem. In each case you will have to keep both chain lines in alignment. The tension of the connecting or synchronizing chain must be maintained as outlined for bicycles without derailleur gearing above, allowing ½ to ¾ in of vertical movement near the middle of the chain. On most tandems this adjustment can be made by means of an excentric mounting bushing for one of the two crank-sets. A close look at it will tell you how to move it so that the axle comes further forward or backward. If no more adjustment is possible, you can remove a set of two links from the chain – but do that only once with any one chain, since shortening the chain any further will add to the wear of the chainwheels: replace the chain instead. If the synchronizing chainwheels are worn, replace them with relatively big ones (and install a new, longer chain): I'd say 36 teeth is a minimal size to guarantee smooth operation and low wear.

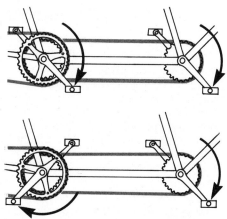

A favorite trick of many touring tandem riders is to off-set the two sets of cranks relative to one-another. Do that (or get back to the regular lined-up arrangement, which just as many riders seem to prefer) either by disconnecting the synchronizing chain and reinstalling it when the cranks are in the desired position relative to each other, or by undoing one set of (cotterless) cranks and reinstalling it in the desired orientation with the chain in place.

7
Derailleur Gearing

Derailleur gearing systems are used almost universally on adult bicycles sold in the USA these days. Unfortunately, the derailleur system deserves much better treatment than it gets from many inexperienced cyclists: it only performs well if it is maintained and adjusted well. To do that, the cyclist should first understand the system as a whole and the way the individual components operate.

The illustration shows a typical derailleur gearing system, consisting of front derailleur, rear derailleur, control cables and shift levers. Alternative positions of the shift levers, as used on different types of bicycles, include handlebar stem, handlebar ends and top of handlebars. The LH shift lever operates the front derailleur and allows the chain to be forced from one chainwheel to the other. On five-speed systems the front derailleur is missing. The RH lever controls the rear derailleur, which shifts the chain from one sprocket to another. A spring-tensioned device in the rear derailleur takes up any slack that comes free when the chain is shifted from the combination *biggest chainwheel, biggest sprocket.* In fact, there should be just a little more slack, so as to allow the chain to 'climb' over the teeth of the biggest chainwheel and sprocket as it is shifted.

The most frequently encountered derailleur problems – improper shifting, often with the chain either being shifted past the outer- or innermost sprocket or chainwheel – can be corrected with simple adjustment of the derailleur, the shift lever or the cable tension. Keeping the various components clean and lubricated, and protecting them against damage, will generally suffice to keep the entire system operating satisfactorily. Just the same, I have also included instructions for removing, installing and overhauling the various components.

Especially when replacing any part of the derailleur system, the limitations of the particular components (e.g. the range of gears for which a particular derailleur is suitable) must be considered: ask in the bike shop to make sure the components in question can be used in combination as you intend. Also refer to the preceding chapter where the interaction of derailleurs and the other components of the drive-train is concerned.

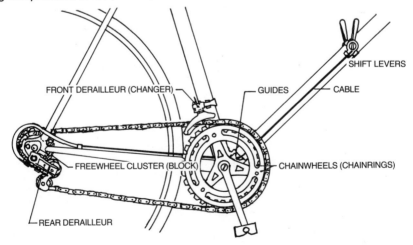

SHIFT LEVERS

FRONT DERAILLEUR (CHANGER) — GUIDES — CABLE

—FREEWHEEL CLUSTER (BLOCK) —CHAINWHEELS (CHAINRINGS)

—REAR DERAILLEUR

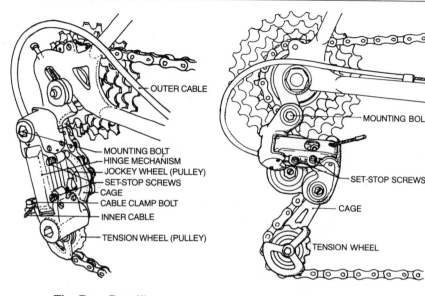

The Rear Derailleur

There are well over a hundred different makes and models of rear derailleurs on the market today, so it should be no surprise that I can't give complete step-by-step instructions for any one model individually. Instead, I shall concentrate on what all rear derailleurs have in common, leaving it to your ingenuiety to figure out the finer details that apply to the particular model used on the bike in question.

Common to all rear derailleurs is a spring-tensioned cage with two little wheels or pulleys over which the chain runs. This cage is attached to a spring-loaded lever mechanism in the shape of an extractable pivoted parallelogram, which keeps it parallel while moving it sideways from one sprocket to the other. Operation is by means of a Bowden cable, consisting of an inner cable, attached to a movable part of the parallelogram linkage, and an outer cable that is anchored to a fixed part of the derailleur. The entire derailleur (including what I just called a 'fixed' part) is free to pivot partway around the fixing bolt with which the entire mechanism is attached to the frame. Play around with the lever a little while observing what happens at the derailleur, as you turn the pedals at the same time, and you will soon get the picture – which is known to be worth a thousand words.

Several adjustments can be carried out on the derailleur. The cable tension must be so adjusted that the derailleur starts moving away from the neutral position, corresponding to the smallest sprocket, when the control lever is moved by a small fraction of its travel range. The 'throw' of the derailleur – i.e. the distance over which the chain can be moved sideways – is adjusted by means of the two set-stop or limit screws. Usually these have little coil springs under their heads to prevent accidental loosening due to vibration. One of these set-stop screws limits the movement towards the right ('outside' or high gear); the other one limits travel towards the center of the bike (the 'inside' or low gear limit adjustment). Screwing the screw in limits travel, unscrewing it increases the range – provided the cable tension allows this much travel.

Some derailleurs, primarily SunTour models, have an additional adjusting screw, which limits the arc of movement of the derailleur around its mounting bolt, to allow the upper one of the two little wheels over which the chain runs (the jockey pulley) to snug up closely to the sprockets, which provides superior shifting response.

The differences between the various makes and models refer to their method of construction and the range of gears they can handle. They may be limited by the biggest rear sprocket or by the difference between highest and lowest gear for which the derailleur's cage can 'wrap up' the amount of chain length that comes free as you change from a combination with big sprocket and chainwheel to a combination with small ones.

As regards construction, both the way the cage pivots and the way the linkage parallelogram pivots can differ from one model to the next. On some types the cage is pivoted at the axis of the jockey pulley; on other models the cage pivot is at some other point on the cage. The linkage may have either a single or double spring. On single spring models the linkage is free to rotate (sometimes limited by a stop screw) around the mounting bolt, whereas on double spring models a coil spring pulls the entire linkage towards the back. These designations are somewhat deceptive, since they refer only to the number of springs that rotate either the cage or the linkage. The additional spring which extends the linkage system outward is thus ignored. So much for the technical details; let's get on with maintenance instructions.

Adjust Rear Derailleur

This adjustment is required when the derailleur does not shift properly, especially when either one or more gears can not be reached, or when the chain is 'dumped', i.e. shifted beyond the smallest or biggest sprocket in the back.

Tools and equipment
☐ small screwdriver
☐ rag (if the chain was dumped)
☐ small wrench to fit cable clamp bolt and pliers (if cable tension must be adjusted beyond the range of the barrel adjuster)

Procedure
1. Set the shift lever in the position for the highest gear (smallest sprocket) and, if necessary, place the chain back on this smallest sprocket. Make sure the shift lever operates properly – tighten if necessary.
2. Check the cable to make sure it will travel freely – replace if necessary.
3. Verify the cable tension: in this position and with the shift lever set appropriately (i.e. pushed all the way forward or, on bar-end shifters, set in line with the end of the handlebars, i.e. up), the cable should be straight, with just the tiniest bit of play; as soon as the shift lever is moved, the cable should tighten and then start to move the derailleur linkage in towards the bike. Correct if necessary, using either the barrel adjuster or the clamp bolt for the inner cable end, while pulling the cable taut with the pliers.
4. Now adjust the distance by which the linkage moves the cage out with the set-stop screws: if it was moved too far out, screw the high range set-stop screw (usually marked H) in a little; if it was not moved out far enough (i.e. if the smallest sprocket was not reached properly), unscrew it a little. If the biggest sprocket was not quite reached, screw the low range set-stop

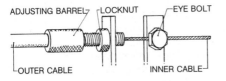

ADJUSTING BARREL — ┌LOCKNUT   ┌EYE BOLT

└OUTER CABLE   INNER CABLE┘

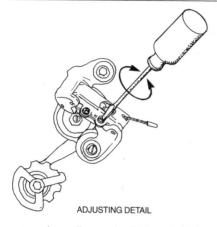

ADJUSTING DETAIL

each of these components to match the others. On cheaper bikes drop-outs without derailleur eye are used; in that case, use a derailleur with an adaptor plate to fit between drop-out and axle nut or quick-release of the same make. Finally, you should be warned that the threaded mounting eyes for derailleur installation may have different types of screw threading (or indeed no screw thread at all), which will further restrict your choice to a compatible model: ask at the bike shop or try it out carefully first.

screw (usually marked L) out; if the chain had been pushed beyond it, screw it in a little.

5. Holding the rear wheel off the ground (or with the bike upside-down, taking adequate care not to damage the brake cables or anything mounted on the handlebars), check all the gears, making any further adjustments that may be required.

Replace Rear Derailleur

This will be required when a derailleur has to be overhauled or is damaged enough to warrant replacing. You may also wish to exchange a derailleur for a model that allows a different range of gearing. In general, I would suggest you try to match the various components of the derailleur system and the drop-outs to which the derailleur is mounted (on bikes with a drop-out with derailleur eye) with products of the same maker, since the manufacturers take great trouble to design

Tools and equipment
☐ wrenches to fit mounting bolt (usually Allen key), cable clamp bolt and pulley axle bolt
☐ small screwdriver
☐ pliers
☐ rag

Removal procedure
1. Set the derailleur for the chain to engage the smallest sprocket.
2. Loosen the cable and remove the short piece of outer cable.
3. Unscrew the axle bolt of the lower pulley over which the chain runs (the tension pulley) and remove the pulley, taking care not to lose any parts. This releases the chain from the derailleur cage – alternately the chain may be opened up and removed. On some derailleurs an open cage, or a cage that can be opened, is used – in those cases you merely take the chain out of the cage.
4. Unscrew the mounting bolt (on models mounted directly to a derailleur eye on the drop-out) or undo the rear wheel axle nut or quick-release (on models with adaptor plate); remove the rear wheel, then loosen the adaptor plate screw and remove the adaptor plate complete with the derailleur.
5. Reinstall the tension pulley in the derailleur cage, if necessary.

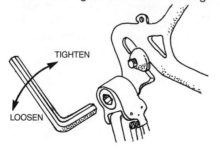

TIGHTEN

LOOSEN

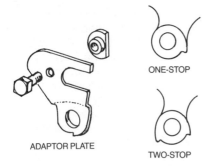

ADAPTOR PLATE

ONE-STOP

TWO-STOP

Installation procedure

1. Ascertain that the derailleur has the right kind of mounting bolt to match the drop-out (or has an adaptor plate), and that the derailleur can handle the gearing range used on the bike.

2. Make sure the inner cable is not frayed and is free to move – replace inner or outer cable if necessary, and lubricate the cable and the shift lever.

3. Make sure the chain is clean and lubricated – clean and lubricate first if necessary. Put the chain on the smallest sprocket (or install after the derailleur has been mounted). Remove the rear wheel if the drop-out has no derailleur eye.

4. Make sure the freewheel and sprockets are clean – clean if necessary.

5. If the chain is installed, remove the axle bolt for the derailleur's tension pulley.

6. On models without a derailleur eye in the drop-out, install the mounting plate with the derailleur in the slot for the rear axle on the RH side, the special nut fitted in the end of the slot, after which the screw is tightened. Now install the rear wheel, lining up the slots in the adaptor plate and the drop-out.

7. On models with a derailleur eye, remove the adaptor plate from the derailleur, if installed. Screw the derailleur in place with the mounting bolt; check that it is free to pivot around the

mounting bolt (on some models against the tension of a spring).

8. Route the chain around the jockey and tension pulleys and install the tension pulley (if removed) – this is easiest to do if you take the chain off the front chainwheel, so that it hangs free. Install the chain again when completed.

9. Pull the inner cable through the outer cable, and clamp the end of the inner cable in the clamp on the derailleur: with the derailleur set for the smallest sprocket and the shift lever in the appropriate position, the cable should be straight but not quite under tension.

10. Carry out the adjustments shown above under *Adjust Rear Derailleur.* Apply some lubrication to the various pivot points, then wipe off excess lubricant.

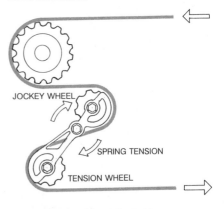

JOCKEY WHEEL

SPRING TENSION

TENSION WHEEL

Overhaul Rear Derailleur

No step-by-step instructions here, due to the great variety of rear derailleurs on the market. Remove the derailleur as described above. Check to make sure nothing is seriously bent and none of the pivots or corresponding bushings are worn so far as to give a 'sloppy' fit. Clean the entire assembly in a mixture of kerosene (paraffin in Britain) and one part in ten of mineral oil, using a small bottle brush. Wipe dry with a clean rag. If necessary, proceed by disassembling the cage and

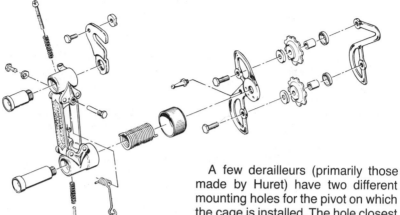

the two pulleys. You may be able to tighten one of the springs if its tension appeared to be insufficient, and you may want to replace the two pulleys if they are seriously worn (either on the outside or at the bearings). If you replace them, I suggest using a type that runs on ball bearings. There is rarely any need or justification to go much further than the work described so far: either cleaning, lubricating and adjusting will do the trick, or nothing will, in which case you should replace the entire unit.

One part that may need close attention is the coil spring which pulls the cage back (and on many models, a similar spring which pulls the derailleur linkage back). Such coil springs are generally contained in a cylindrical housing, which can be opened up by unscrewing a cap with a hexagonal recess. Remove the spring and carefully clean and lubricate the interior as well as the spring itself. Quite commonly, there are two or more different locking positions for the coil, so it can be tightened by placing the end in the other position – details vary between different models, but once you know what the idea is, you'll be able to figure out what to do.

A few derailleurs (primarily those made by Huret) have two different mounting holes for the pivot on which the cage is installed. The hole closest to the outside should be selected when the derailleur will be used with wide-range gearing (big largest sprocket); the other hole is used for narrow-range gearing, i.e. when the largest sprocket is of moderate or small size. The appropriate sprocket sizes will be engraved near the holes.

Maintenance of Indexed Derailleur Systems

Since 1986 there has been a veritable revolution in derailleur gearing with the introduction of high-quality indexed shifting systems. Most bicycles sold in the US these days are equipped with such a system for the rear derailleur. No more fiddling to find the right position of the lever for a gear change, no more missed changes – until the system gets out of adjustment. . . .

To assure troublefree operation of the indexed system, make sure you do not mix components: use shift levers, derailleurs and freewheel blocks from the same manufacturer. Use only the special heavier cable and regularly check the adjustment of the cable tension. The cable must be taut when the highest gear (largest chainwheel, smallest sprocket) is engaged, adjusting by means of the barrel adjuster, as described above. Replace the cable annually, and lubricate it slightly once a month, wiping off any excess lubricant afterwards.

If the system fails to shift properly, you may solve the problem temporarily by selecting the friction mode — a selection lever on the shifter is marked correspondingly. You now have a regular gearing system that can be adjusted as described on page 62 if overshifting or undershifting occurs. This is the quick roadside repair solution.

For a more permanent correction, adjust the entire system as follows, with the wheel raised off the ground, turning the cranks forward while executing the necessary shifts:

Adjusting procedure:

1. Select the highest gear (large chainring, smallest sprocket) in friction mode, and adjust the high gear as described on page 62 for a regular derailleur.

2. Still in friction mode, select the lowest gear (small chainring, biggest sprocket), and adjust the low gear.

3. Select the highest gear again, then switch to index shifting mode.

4. Shift to the second position (next bigger sprocket). If the derailleur does not follow, increase cable tension by means of the adjusting barrel on the rear derailleur or the shift lever until it does.

5. If the derailleur overshifts, slacken the cable a little by means of the adjusting barrel until the shift is executed correctly.

6. With the chain still on the second smallest chainring, tighten the adjusting barrel until the chain noisily runs against the 3rd sprocked, then back off until the chain runs silently.

7. Try out all the gears, making any further adjustments that may be necessary.

Note: If this does not solve your problem, the shifter mechanism may be worn so much that it should be replaced. Alternately, the drop-out, the frame or the derailleur may be bent. If necessary, let a bike shop mechanic check it and carry out any repair that may be required

The Front Derailleur

This fellow is quite a bit simpler than the rear derailleur. It consists of a simple cage, through which the chain runs, and a linkage mechanism to move the cage with the chain sideways. The whole thing is (usually) clamped around the seat tube, although it is becoming more and more fashionable on expensive machines to mount it on a special boss which is brazed to the seat tube – in that case you are locked into models made by the same manufacturer.

Almost any front derailleur will shift satisfactorily if the difference between the larger and the smaller chainwheels is up to about 14 teeth. For larger differences – especially for wide-range gearing with triple chainwheels, as used on most mountain bikes, tandems and true touring bicycles – you may need a special wide-range model, which has a longer and still adequately

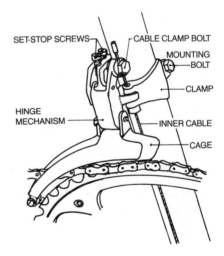

strong cage. People who work in bike shops ought to be able to tell you which types are suitable for the kind of gearing you want to use. To adjust, there are set-stop screws to limit cage travel.

Most front derailleurs are what is referred to in the catalogs as 'low normal', meaning that the spring tension pulls the derailleur towards the smaller (inner) chainwheel, which gives the lower gear. For all these models the LH shift lever is pushed forward when the chain is on the small chainwheel and pulled back to put it on the large chainwheel. A few models (mainly by SunTour) operate the other way round, which is referred to as 'high normal'. Make sure you know which type you have, so you don't try to adjust the thing incorrectly.

Adjust Front Derailleur

Adjustment of the front derailleur will be required when the chain does not engage one of the chainwheels properly or is shifted beyond the chainwheel. In addition, adjustment will be required after the crankset has been replaced. If another size large chainwheel is installed, the mounting point should be revised; this adjustment is covered under installation procedure in the description *Replace Front Derailleur* below.

Tools and equipment
□ small screwdriver
□ rag (if chain was dumped)
□ small wrench to fit cable clamp bolt and pliers (if cable tension must be adjusted, unless a barrel adjuster is provided, which is rarely the case)

Procedure
1. In case the chain had come off, put it back first.
2. Make sure the cable moves freely and the shift lever does not slip; correct if necessary.

3. Set the shift lever for the normal position, i.e. forward (bar-end shifter: horizontal), corresponding to the normal gear, which is usually the small chainwheel, making sure the chain is indeed on the appropriate chainwheel. Put the chain on the smallest sprocket in the back.

4. Adjust cable tension so that the cable is just straight in this position: it should tighten and then start to move as soon as the shift lever is moved. If required, pull the cable taut with the pliers, while loosening and then tightening the cable clamp bolt.

5. Using the set-stop screws, adjust the amount of travel of the front derailleur cage: if the chain was pushed too far beyond the smaller chainwheel, turn the low range set-stop screw (usually marked L) in; if it was not moved far enough, turn it out a little. If it was pushed too far beyond the larger chainwheel, turn the high range set-stop screw (usually marked H) in; if it was not moved far enough, turn it out a little.

BRAZED-ON FRONT DERAILLEUR (CHANGER) MOUNT

6. Keeping the rear wheel off the ground (or with the bike upside-down, providing fragile items on the handlebars are protected), check all the gears and make any further adjustments that may be required.

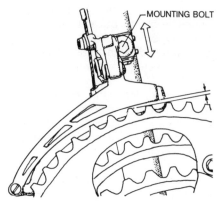

MOUNTING BOLT

Replace Front Derailleur

You may want to replace a derailleur if its range is inadequate for the gearing you want to use or if it is damaged. Follow the same instructions to remove and reinstall before and after overhauling.

Tools and equipment
□ wrenches to fit mounting bolt and cable clamp bolt
□ pliers
□ screwdriver
□ rag
□ chain rivet tool (unless the cage has a screw which makes it easier to open up the cage than it would be to remove the chain)

Removal procedure
1. Place shift lever and derailleur in the normal position (usually on the smaller chainwheel) and place the chain on a small sprocket in the back.
2. Remove the cable at the derailleur, removing any piece of outer cable that may be used there (rarely the case these days, since the cable is run over a special guide at the bottom bracket).
3. Free the chain from the cage, either by removing the screw and bushing in the cage or by opening up the chain itself. Reinstall screw and bushing if needed.
4. Unscrew the mounting bolt and remove the derailleur complete with its clamp.

Installation procedure
1. Make sure the derailleur has the right capacity for the gearing chosen and that it has the right kind of mount-

ing (if the frame has a brazed-on front derailleur mount, it must usually be of the same make).
2. Make sure the derailleur itself and the cable and shift lever operate properly; replace and/or lubricate as appropriate.
3. Either separate the chain or open up the cage of the derailleur to guide the chain through it, then reassemble chain or derailleur cage. Route the chain as shown in the illustration under *Rear Derailleur* above.
4. Install the front derailleur on the seat tube, removing the clamp if a brazed-on boss for derailleur installation is provided. See the illustration for the right position: about 1.5–3 mm (1/16–1/8 in) clearance between the top of the chainwheel teeth and the bottom of the cage. Place the cage parallel to the chainwheel.
5. Install the cable, keeping it taut with the pliers.
6. Adjust the set-stop screws as outlined under *Adjust Front Derailleur* above. Apply some lubrication to the cable and the various guides and pivot points; then wipe off any excess lubricant.

Overhaul Front Derailleur

Once more, no detailed instructions: the most important part is removal, installation and adjustment, as described in detail in the instructions above. Generally, it will be enough to remove the derailleur, wash it out in a mixture of solvent and some mineral oil, using a small bottle brush to get in all the nooks and crannies, followed by reinstallation and adjustment. Here is an exploded view of just one particular type – if only to give you an idea of what the thing might look like if taken apart completely, if you want to go that far.

Derailleur Controls

Quite often what is wrong with derailleur gearing is not so much a problem in the derailleur mechanism itself, but rather one of the controls: shift levers, cables and guides. The first thing to check, therefore, should be whether the controls are operating correctly. Check whether the shift levers are adjusted tightly (the little wing nut or other screw on top should be tightened), whether levers and guides are attached properly, so they don't slip when force is applied to the cables, and whether the cables themselves are in good condition: not frayed, corroded, dirty or pinched. Any sections of outer cable used (mainly when the shift levers are installed on the handlebars, but also at the rear derailleur) should run in a smooth curve, yet must be as short as possible, consistent with extraneous movements. Both

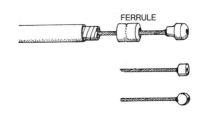

FERRULE

inner and outer cables should be cut off carefully to avoid frayed ends in the inner cable and the formation of a hook on the outer cable.

Several different shift levers are in use, mounted on the down tube, the handlebar stem, the handlebar ends or on top of the handlebars. Some models have a simple friction washer, whereas other types are equipped with an ingenious ratchet mechanism, which makes for low shifting resistance. In general, it is best to match derailleur and shift lever, since some derailleurs require more cable movement to operate them than certain levers can provide. Special derailleurs with fixed or indexed gear positions should always be used with the appropriate shift levers, on which these same positions are marked, and generally with the special cable supplied with the system.

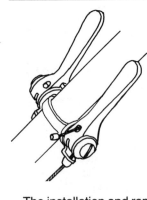

The installation and replacement of most shift levers and cables does not warrant detailed instructions. As long as you tighten the various parts properly, lubricate the cable, and cut it off carefully, all you need do is look at the shift lever to determine what kind of cable nipple is required and how it is inserted. Adjust the cable tension with the gear in the normal position (and the chain in the appropriate gear), so that it is nearly taut and starts to tighten and move as soon as the shifter is moved. Cut off the cable about 25 mm (1 in) beyond the point where it is clamped. It is preferable to solder the end with an electric soldering iron (if you have one: you will need a model that is rated at least 60 watt) to prevent fraying. You may use a pair of sharp diagonal cutters or a special cable cutter. The shift levers may be installed on brazed-on bosses on the frame – here you are once more tied in to install only levers by the same manufacturer.

Replace Bar-End Shift Levers

This is the only type of shift lever that requires special attention when installing. There are two basic types: with the cable routed through the handlebars or the cable routed outside the handlebars. The former require holes drilled in the handlebars, for which reason (or rather the resulting loss of strength) I would advise you to steer clear of them. If your handlebars have the holes pre-drilled, you may use that type, but I'd certainly advise you to get a model for external cable routing, rather than drill your own holes. Disturbing though this may be, you will largely have to follow this same procedure just to replace the handlebar tape.

Tools and equipment
☐ wrenches to fit cable clamp bolt at derailleur and locknut on lever pivot bolt

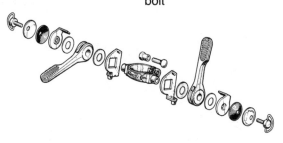

□ pliers
□ medium screwdriver
□ Allen key to fit internal mounting bolt
□ lubricant

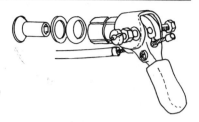

Disassembly procedure

1. Place bike in the gear corresponding to the normal position for both derailleurs (always small sprocket in the rear, usually small chainwheel in the front).

2. Loosen the cable at the derailleur and free it from the guides and sections of inner cable as far as possible.

3. Unscrew the lever pivot bolt and remove the bushing and the locknut on the other side.

4. Remove the lever with the two washers, then remove the inner cable.

5. With the Allen key, loosen the internal mounting bolt, turning to the right; this will loosen the expander plug that holds the lever assembly mounting body in the end of the handlebars.

6. Now remove the inner cable (if run through the handlebars); remove handlebar tape and outer cable in case you want to replace it and it is run outside the handlebars.

Installation Procedure

1. If the cable is to be run outside the handlebars, old handlebar tape and the old outer cable may have to be removed first.

2. Check to make sure the chain is in the gear that corresponds to the normal position for both derailleurs (small sprocket in the rear, usually small chainwheel in the front).

3. Route the outer cable along the handlebar the way it interferes least, but always at the bottom near the end

where the lever is to be installed; attach with short pieces of adhesive tape (or run the cables through the handlebars if these have holes).

4. Wrap handlebar tape around the handlebars, as outlined in Chapter 4.

5. Loosely assemble the control body without the lever (i.e. expander plug, mounting bolt and mounting body), with the slot for the lever in line with the outer cable facing down. Tighten the mounting bolt by turning it to the left with the Allen key.

6. Slightly lubricate the lever bushing and contact surfaces, then install the lever, placing washers on either side. Tighten the pivot screw and the locknut.

7. Lubricate the cable, then thread the cable through the lever in such a way that the nipple will lie in the recess in the lever; now push the cable through the outer cable, over the guides, and attach to the derailleur. Alternately, you may prefer to thread the inner cable through the lever and the outer cable before installing the lever in the mounting unit — it always must be done this way when the cable is run through the handlebars.

8. Place the lever in the horizontal position and pull the cable taut with the pliers at the derailleur, then attach firmly. Make any adjustments as described under *Derailleur Maintenance* elsewhere in this chapter.

8
Hub Gearing

Although hub gearing is not used as extensively as derailleur gearing these days, a separate chapter does seem justified, since most problems and maintenance operations are quite different from those encountered with derailleur gearing. The illustration shows the various components of the system. A gearing mechanism is built into the rear wheel hub, offering the choice of (usually) three different gears: a normal gear in which the wheel turns at the same speed as the rear sprocket, a low gear in which the wheel turns slower, and a high gear in which it turns faster than the sprocket. The mechanism is controlled by means of a shifter on the handlebars via a flexible cable, attached to the control rod that runs through the rear hub axle.

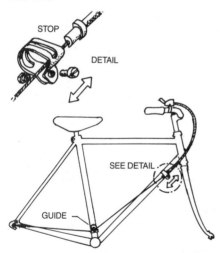

Several variations are possible, such as a two-speed system (normal and high gear only), operated by pedalling back briefly, and a five-speed system, operated with a double set of control levers. In addition, the hub may be combined with a built-in coaster brake (the two-speed system nearly always, sometimes also the three-

speed model), a drum brake, or a hub generator to supply electricity for the lighting system. Finally, there are systems which combine hub and derailleur gearing, which have the advantage of replacing the (for most beginners hard-to-use) front derailleur by a simple hub gear, combined with five or six sprockets for use with a rear derailleur. The ratio between the various gears is always fixed, but the range may be changed for a higher or lower one by exchanging the sprocket.

In general, hub gearing is less trouble-prone than derailleur gearing. In normal use and with minimal lubrication, the hub itself will often outlive the bike. However, since these systems are often chosen by riders who have very limited technical ambition, they are often so poorly maintained, lubricated and adjusted, that they still don't work right. Nine times out of ten, the problem can be eliminated quickly with lubrication and adjustment. In most of the remaining cases repairing or replacing the shifter or the control cable will do the trick. It is a rare case indeed that requires overhauling the hub gear mechanism itself.

As was the case with derailleur gearing, understanding how the system works will ease proper operation and maintenance. Hang up the bike by seat and handlebars (or place it upside-down, supporting the handlebars in such a way that nothing gets damaged and the shift lever can be operated), and work the gears while turning the pedals slowly. Observe what happens to the speed of the rear wheel as you shift from one gear to the other. Note how, shifting to a lower gear, the lever is pulled in and the cable tension pulls the control device a little further out of the hub axle (or in the case of the so-called bell crank operator, as used by Shimano, how

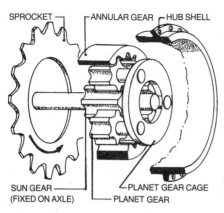

SPROCKET — ANNULAR GEAR — HUB SHELL

SUN GEAR — (FIXED ON AXLE) — PLANET GEAR CAGE — PLANET GEAR

bell-crank) once a month, or whenever the bike has not been used for some time. This is also the first step to take if it malfunctions – quite often it will solve the problem. Occasionally the control system should be adjusted – especially when shifting appears to be imprecise or unpredictable, and whenever the rear wheel has been removed. The shift lever and the various guides over which the cable runs may also need some oil; the same goes for any section of the cable that runs through a piece of outer cable.

the same thing is achieved via a hinge mechanism at the hub).

Inside the hub is a mechanism consisting of a fixed sun gear, a hollow annular gear inside the hub shell, and a set of little planet gears that rotate between the two, making contact with both the sun gear and the annular gear. The control rod inside the hub axle is connected to a set of clutches that connect the planet gears and the annular gear in different methods. In the normal gear the planet gears are by-passed and the annular gear is connected with the hub shell, so the sprocket drives the annular gear (and with it the entire wheel) directly at the same speed. In the high gear the planet gears are fixed in such a way that they drive the annular gear faster than the sprocket. In the low gear the planet gears turn backward and drive the hub shell slower than the sprocket. Four- and five-speed models comprise double sets of sun, planet and annular gears.

Hub Gear Lubrication

By way of regular maintenance, all hub gears require lubrication. Pour 10 to 20 drops of heavy mineral oil (e.g. SAE 60 motor oil) into the oiling nipple, and a few more drops on the control rod activating mechanism (chain or

Adjust Sturmey-Archer or SunTour Three-Speed Hub

Sturmey-Archer and SunTour hub gears are not merely similar: they are identical, except that Sturmey-Archer, who makes them all, prints a different name on the ones sold to SunTour. Unlike most three-speed hubs made by Fichtel & Sachs (Torpedo), these hubs have a neutral position between two gears, so maladjustment is usually evidenced by complete slipping out of gear. Whenever this happens, or when irregular resistance is felt, adjust as follows:

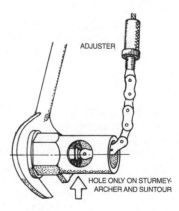

ADJUSTER

HOLE ONLY ON STURMEY-ARCHER AND SUNTOUR

Tools and equipment
☐ usually none required (pliers may be required if mechanism is too tight)

Procedure

1. Check to make sure the cable and control lever operate freely – correct if necessary.

2. Put the control lever in the normal (N or 2) position, for the intermediate gear, while turning the cranks either forward or backward at least half a turn.

3. Check inside the hole in the RH axle nut whether the picture shown on page 73 applies: the end of the control rod should line up exactly with the axle end.

4. If required, adjust the adjusting mechanism between the little control chain and the control cable until the situation described under point 3 applies: loosen the round locknut while holding the adjusting barrel, screw the adjusting barrel in or out while holding the threaded end of the pin on the chain, finally tighten the locknut again while holding the adjusting barrel in place.

5. If adjustment is not possible, it may be necessary to replace either the control rod with control chain (just screw it out, after disconnecting at the cable; screw the new rod in – but not too tightly, so that the control chain is not twisted).

Note: When replacing any gear hub part, I highly recommend buying only original (more expensive, but indeed far superior) Sturmey-Archer spares – that will prevent all sorts of misery, even though it costs a little more.

Adjust Sturmey-Archer Five-Speed Hub

This little goody has a control on either side of the hub. Older models may have a bell crank mechanism on the LH side – see the description for adjusting the Shimano three-speed hub for details. In general, adjustment is similar to that described above for Sturmey-Archer three-speed hubs. First set the LH control in the normal posi-

tion, and adjust the RH mechanism as described above. Then pull the shift lever for the LH mechanism in, pedal half a turn, and loosen the LH adjuster; turn the pedals once more, and finally adjust the LH adjuster until all slack is taken up. Try out all gears while cycling, and make any further adjustments that may be necessary.

Adjust Fichtel & Sachs Three-Speed Hub

Many of the models made by this company (some are called 'Torpedo') have a built-in coaster brake. Newer models of this type no longer have a neutral position, which eliminates the danger of losing control of the brake if the hub is maladjusted. Older models have a 'neutral' mark on the shift lever between 2nd and 3rd gear, which may be used to adjust; however, the following procedure can be used for all models.

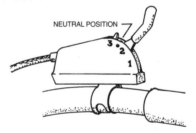

NEUTRAL POSITION

Tools and equipment

☐ usually none required (pliers may be needed if the adjuster is particularly tight)

Procedure

1. Make sure the control cable and shift lever operate properly.

2. Select the high gear (3 or H) position on the shift lever, while pedalling forward with the rear wheel lifted off the ground by at least one half revolution.

3. In this position the cable should be just straight, but not yet under strain:

adjust in or out (as described for Sturmey-Archer gear above), and keep in place with the round locknut once the correct position has been found.

Note: If adjusting won't do the trick, the control rod with chain may have to be replaced, again using only the manufacturer's original spares, rather than cheaper (and inferior) unbranded equipment.

Adjust Shimano Three-Speed Hub

This manufacturer uses a bell crank, as shown in the illustration. This is a kind of hinge mechanism, screwed onto the longer end of the hollow axle in which the control rod runs. In the window in the bell crank a letter N appears centered when the mechanism is correctly set for the normal gear (second gear). Adjustment in all other respects is exactly as described above for Sturmey-Archer three-speeds.

If required, the rear wheel can be removed without disturbing the bell crank, since the axle nut has enough free screw thread on the axle between it and the bell crank's locknut. When the bell crank has been removed for some reason or other, or when the rear wheel has been removed, make sure it is installed in such a way that the plane over which the bell crank turns is in line with the cable pull. Make

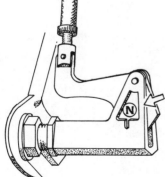

any corrections necessary by loosening the locknut, turning the bell crank as appropriate, and then tightening the locknut against it, while holding the bell crank firmly in place.

Hub Gear Controls

With the exception of the two-speed hubs, which are operated by pedalling backward, and which can not be adjusted externally, all hub gearing systems are operated similarly by means of shift levers with fixed positions for the gears via cables. These run over stops and guides, and partway through an outer cable (between the shift lever and the first stop on the frame). The Sturmey-Archer five-speed hub comes with stem-mounted shifters, which I consider both potentially dangerous and inconvenient to use. It should be no problem to replace these by ordinary shifters as used on three-speed hubs, following the instructions for shift lever replacement below.

The maintenance required on hub gear controls is replacing the cable or the shifter when the cable no longer runs smoothly or is frayed, or when the shifter fails to maintain the gear properly. Sometimes the shifter can be rescued by disassembling and bending in the spring that stops the mechanism in certain positions, or by filing the 'teeth' in the plate that the spring rests in – use your ingenuity, since I can't give detailed instructions for such rare jobs. When working on the controls, also make sure the stops and guides are securely fixed in their proper location. You may want to modify that position slightly if the adjustment range at the hub has been exceeded.

Replace Hub Gear Control Cable

Although my experience indicates that the shift lever itself will have to be replaced more frequently, and is usually supplied complete with cable, you may still have to replace the cable alone. At the same time, make sure the guides and stops are in good condition, and replace them if necessary.

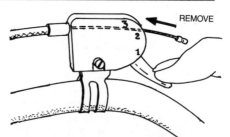

Tools and equipment
☐ usually none required (pliers may be needed if adjuster is too tight; screwdriver and wrench may be required if stops or guides have to be moved; pliers may be needed to shorten the cable and to attach a nipple if the cable is not available in the correct length)

Removal procedure
1. Place the bike in the highest gear, so there is no strain on the cable.
2. Undo the cable at the adjusting mechanism near the hub; take care not to lose the control rod with its chain on models without bell crank.
3. Pull the cable through the stops and guides.
4. Push the control lever in all the way (i.e. beyond the low gear position); this allows pushing the cable nipple free with the cable, pushing *against* the 'remove' arrow in the illustration; now the cable with the nipple can be pulled out in the direction of the 'remove' arrow in the illustration.

Installation procedure
1. Ascertain that the new cable has the right length, the right kind of nipple and has the right outer cable, guides and adjusting attachment to fit the components of the bike. If the exact type is not available, you may cut off the nipple, install the various correct parts from the old cable, perhaps shorten the outer cable, if required, and

clamp a separate nipple (this is a brass bushing, available separately in the bike store) on in the right position. Adaptor fittings are available to use one type of cable with a hub control mechanism designed for another cable.
2. Push the handle in as far beyond the 1 or L position as possible, and insert the nipple with the cable from the opposite end; release the lever and pull the cable back until the nipple is caught in place.
3. Route the cable over the guides (which may have to be moved somewhat to accommodate the new cable's length), and attach the adjuster end to the end of the control chain or the bell crank.
4. Adjust the gears in accordance with the instructions given above for the make and model in question.

Replace Hub Gear Shift Lever
No detailed step-by-step instructions here; it's done exactly the same way as described above for cable replacement. All you need in addition, is a screwdriver to remove and install the clamp with which the lever is mounted on the handlebars. Don't forget to adjust the gears after the unit has been installed.

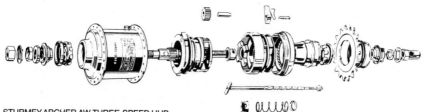

STURMEY-ARCHER AW THREE-SPEED HUB

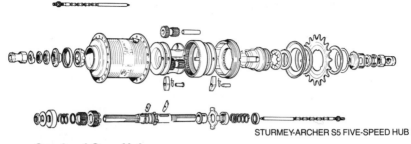

STURMEY-ARCHER S5 FIVE-SPEED HUB

Overhaul Gear Hub

Although three-speed hubs (and even the relatively expensive five-speed) are not very expensive as sophisticated bicycle components go, overhauling may still be worthwhile when adjusting and lubrication does not solve the problem. The reason to do this lies mainly in the high cost (or the time-consuming work) involved in rebuilding the wheel, which will be necessary when replacing the hub. Yet it is beyond the scope of this book to describe this job in detail for each model separately.

In fact, it will be smarter to merely go about it systematically, referring to the various illustrations included on these pages. Roughly be guided by the following initial procedure steps:

1. Undo the control cable at the hub, and remove the wheel from the bike.

2. Remove the control rod or the bell crank.

3. Place the wheel down flat in front of you, the chain side up.

4. Remove the sprocket, as described in Chapter 6, *The Drive Train*.

5. Remove the locknut and the lock washer.

6. Remove the bearing cone and the parts that become accessible.

And now you're on your own, because things get different for the various models. Just work systematically, and if necessary make notes as to the sequence in which things were installed, so you can later get it back together. If it's any consolation, this is the way I go about it myself, and I've always been able to get the hub back in working order eventually. Replace any damaged parts and lubricate before reassembling. See the description in Chapter 6, *The Drive-Train* for instructions on installing the freewheel mechanism. Adjust the bearings carefully. Finally, when you have reinstalled the wheel, proceed as for adjusting, described previously for the make and model in question.

TWO-SPEED HUB WITH COASTER BRAKE

9
The Wheels

In this chapter all repair and maintenance work on the wheels will be covered. I suggest you take a close look at the bicycle wheel first – that will help you understand the work that may be required better. The wheel consists of a hub, a 'network' of spokes, and a rim, on which the tire is mounted. The bicycle wheel is an exceptionally clever device, since the construction with the tensioned wire spokes makes it possible to carry a lot of weight in comparison to the wheel's remarkably low weight, even over rough surfaces and at high speeds.

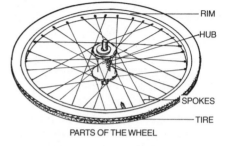

PARTS OF THE WHEEL

The Hub

The bicycle wheel hub consists of a set of ball bearings mounted on a central axle, which is fixed in the bicycle's frame (rear wheel) or fork (front wheel), and a hub shell with flat flanges with holes to which the spokes are attached. The axle may be held in the bike by means of axle nuts or by means of a quick-release lever. In the latter case the axle is hollow and a thin spindle with a cam-operated lever on one end and a screwed-on thumb nut on the other end allows tightening the hub in place. Neither system is inherently superior: since the advent of mountain bikes, components with nuts and solid axles are once more available in the same high quality as exist with quick-releases.

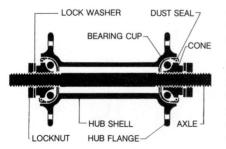

The rear axle (except in the case of a few special models) has screw thread for installation of a freewheel mechanism, or double threading for installation of a fixed wheel and a lockring. Several different threading standards are in use, so the different components (hub, freewheel, sprocket, lockring) should be bought with care to ascertain that they have matching thread. The other factors to consider are the number of spoke holes, which should match the number of spoke holes in the wheel rim, and the overlocknut width of the assembly, which should match the dimensions of the frame or the front fork. This dimension should – in the case of the rear wheel – be consistent with the type of freewheel assembly used (5, 6 or 7 sprockets, in either normal or 'compact' versions). Normal over-locknut dimensions are 100 mm for the front wheel and 120 mm for the rear wheel with five sprockets, 125 mm with six sprockets and 130 mm with seven sprockets and some especially wide hubs, e.g. as used on tandems and some mountain bikes.

Many hubs exist in two versions: high flange and low flange (in Britain called big and small flange, respectively). High flange hubs do not have a real advantage with regards to strength or rigidity (whatever you may have read elsewhere). Consequently, I suggest choosing the lighter and usually slightly cheaper low flange hubs when replacing hub and spokes. Whenever the old spokes can be reused, you should replace the hub with a model of the same flange type, since for most spoking patterns the required spoke lengths will be different. Replacing the hub becomes a matter of spoking the wheel, which will be covered in a separate section of this chapter. In the following instructions hub bearing maintenance and wheel removal and installation will be covered.

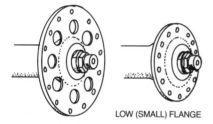

LOW (SMALL) FLANGE

HIGH (LARGE) FLANGE

Remove and Install Wheel with Quick-Release

Yes, it can be done without instructions, but it'll be easier if you follow these steps.

Tools and equipment
□ for rear wheel only: rag

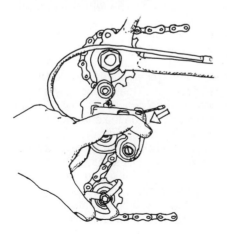

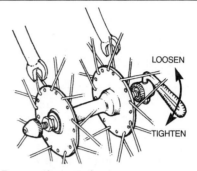

LOOSEN

TIGHTEN

Removal procedure

1. If it's the rear wheel, select the highest gear (smallest sprocket); then turn bike upside-down (taking the usual precautions not to damage anything on the handlebars) or hang it up off the ground.

2. Release the brake (with brake quick-release, if available, or with the adjusting barrel for cable tension) far enough so the tire will clear the brake blocks.

3. Twist the quick-release lever in the 'open' position, and pull the wheel out. If it's the rear wheel of a derailleur bike, hold back the rear derailleur and the chain, so it does not interfere with the sprocket.

Installation procedure

1. If it's a rear wheel, make sure the rear derailleur is set for the smallest sprocket, the front derailleur for the smallest chainwheel. Turn the bike upside-down (taking the usual precautions) or hang it up.

2. Make sure the brakes are open far enough to allow the tire to pass through.

3. Make sure the quick-release lever on the hub is set in the 'open' position, with the thumb nut unscrewed far enough to allow the drop-outs or fork-ends to fit.

4. Push the wheel into position, holding back the chain and derailleur on the rear wheel, then fitting the chain over the sprocket, before releasing the derailleur.

5. Center the wheel at the rim be-tween the brake blocks or the fork blades or stays, and make sure the hub is seated fully in the drop-outs or fork-ends.

6. Move the quick-release lever into the 'closed' position. You should feel a definite resistance and a locking ac-tion: if too tight or too loose, open the lever again, adjust the thumb nut in or out accordingly, and try again. A loose rear wheel could be pulled askew and cause high resistance.

7. Correct any adjustments that were affected: brakes (don't forget to tighten the brake quick-release) and derailleur.

Remove and Install Wheel with Axle Nuts

Tools and equipment
□ wrench to fit axle nuts
□ if rear wheel: rag
□ if wheel with hub brake (coaster brake, drum brake, disc brake, band brake): screwdriver and/or wrench to release the brake arm attachment to the stay or fork blade
□ if it's a bike with stirrup (or roller lever) brake: wrench and/or screw-driver to release the brake
□ if it's the rear wheel on a bike with an enclosed gear case: tools to open gear case in the back.

Removal procedure
1. On rear wheel of any bike with derailleur gearing, place the derailleur in the gear with the smallest sprocket in the back and the smallest chain-wheel in the front.

WASHER

NUT

NUT WITH INTEGRAL WASHER

2. If it's the rear wheel, or if any parts complicate the job (e.g. special brake or parts attached to the wheel axle), place the bike upside-down (taking care to protect anything on the handle-bars) or hang it up off the ground.

3. Adjust the brakes (usually with quick-release) to clear the tire; remove or loosen any other parts that interfere with wheel removal (e.g. hub gear control, accessories mounted on the axle, special brakes).

4. Loosen the axle nuts by at least two full turns on both sides of the hub; remove them completely where any-thing else is mounted on the axles.

5. Remove the wheel; on a rear wheel with derailleur gearing, hold back the derailleur with the chain to clear the sprocket; on a front wheel with wheel locators, bend out the fork (if mounted inside) to clear them, or remove them (if mounted outside). On Dutch utility bikes (but also e.g. many bikes made in China or India) chain tensioners are used, clamped be-tween the hub and the drop-outs, which then point back: loosen to free from the drop-out, so you can first push the wheel forward to take the chain off the sprocket, then withdraw backward.

Installation procedure
1. Proceed as for wheel with quick-release, except that you tighten the axle nuts, making sure the lock wash-ers (if not integral with the nuts) are installed between the drop-outs or fork-ends (or anything mounted there) and the nuts. Tighten securely, since a loose wheel would slip out of align-ment and rub on the chain stay, caus-ing a high resistance.

2. Install all the many parts that may on one bike or the other have to be installed, as detailed in the tools list and the removal instruction above.

3. Make all adjustments necessary (brakes, gears, chain tension).

Adjust Wheel Hub

Although it is often possible to carry out this adjustment while the wheel is still on the bike, it is customary to remove the wheel from the bike first. This description assumes the wheel has been removed.

Tools and equipment
☐ two cone wrenches to fit the specific size cone of the wheel bearings (only one required if the wheel is mounted with axle nuts and is not removed from the bike)
☐ wrench to fit locknut

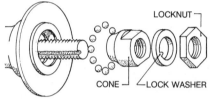

Procedure
1. Loosen locknut on one side of the hub, countering at the cone on the *opposite* side of the hub (if axle nuts and wheel held in bike, first loosen the axle nut on the side you will adjust, opposite the chain, only – this way you need not counter while loosening the locknut).
2. Free the keyed lockwasher between cone and locknut slightly.
3. Tighten or loosen the cone as appropriate: when tightening, counter at the opposite *locknut;* when loosening, counter at the opposite *cone* (not required if axle nuts and wheel held in bike). The correct adjustment allows the wheel to turn freely, yet without any play or slack in the bearing. If this adjustment can not be achieved, proceed to the overhauling instructions below.
4. Tighten the locknut; check once more for correct operation per point 3 above, making any further adjustments that may be required.
5. If the wheel had been kept in the bike, don't forget to tighten it properly.

Overhaul Hub

I suggest doing this work at least once a year, twice if you ride a lot both summer and winter. It's also the job to carry out when adjustment will not return the hub to smooth operation. Even an extensive overhaul – perhaps replacing all internals (only possible on models for which such spares are available, such as Campagnolo) is worthwhile, since it will save you the trouble of rebuilding the entire wheel, as will be necessary to replace the hub. The wheel must be removed from the bike in order to overhaul the hub. On a rear wheel, remove the freewheel from the hub as well.

Tools and equipment
☐ two cone wrenches of the same size
☐ wrench to fit locknuts
☐ bearing grease
☐ rag

Disassembly procedure
1. Remove the locknut on one side, countering at the cone on the opposite side.
2. Remove the keyed lock washer.
3. Remove the cone, again countering at the cone on the opposite side.
4. Use the rag to catch the bearing balls, as you withdraw the axle from the hub with the cone and locknut still in place on one side.
5. Clean and inspect all parts. Replace the balls and any other parts that are corroded, pitted, grooved or otherwise damaged (e.g. a bent axle: check whether it is bent by rolling it over a smooth, level surface). Unless you find the bearing cups must be replaced, leave the dust caps and the bearing cups themselves in the hub. If you must replace them, have that done by a bike mechanic who has a special tool for that job. Before you do, check whether spares are indeed available for the hub in question. Hubs with cartridge bearings vary in their

design; some can be similarly maintained, others can not – inquire at the bike shop.

Assembly procedure

1. Make sure all parts – both old and new – are in perfect condition, cleaned and lubricated.

2. When replacing the bearing cups or cartridge bearings, have that done for you by a bike mechanic, who can also install the dust caps.

3. Place the cone, lock washer and locknut on one side of the axle – on a solid axle, leave 25 mm (1 in) of the axle thread protruding beyond the locknut; on a hollow axle (quick-release), leave 5–6 mm (a little less than ¼ in) protruding; in each case include the appropriate spacers on the freewheel side of the rear hub. Tighten cone and locknut against one another.

4. Fill the bearing cups (or the cartridge bearings) with bearing grease; put the bearing balls in the cups (one less than the maximum number that might seem to fit in at a pinch).

5. Insert the axle into the hub, making sure it's done the right way round on the rear wheel hub (spacers on the freewheel side), taking care not to lose any bearing balls in the process.

6. Install the cone on the other side, followed by the keyed lock washer and the locknut.

7. Adjust as outlined above under *Adjust Wheel Hub.* If required, make

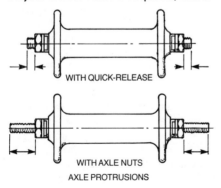

WITH QUICK-RELEASE

WITH AXLE NUTS

AXLE PROTRUSIONS

any corrections to the position of the cones and locknuts either side of the hub, so they protrude equally far both sides, except that the rear axle on the freewheel side of a bike with derailleur mounted on a separate adaptor plate may protrude about 3 mm (⅛ in) further than it does on the other side.

8. Check to make sure each set of cone and locknut is tightened and all bearings are properly adjusted.

The Rim

Bicycle rims come in various designs, materials and widths to match the particular tire used on the bike. Almost universally used on all bicycles other than out-and-out racing machines and the very crudest utility bikes, are rims of the Endrick design. Tubular tires used on racing bikes require Sprint rims; the fat tires on some utility bikes are mounted on Westwood rims.

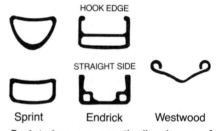

HOOK EDGE

STRAIGHT SIDE

Sprint   Endrick   Westwood

Sprint rims are practically always of aluminum; Westwood rims are always of steel; Endrick rims may be either aluminum or steel. Aluminum rims are far preferable, since they are not only lighter (though equally strong) and better resistant against corrosion, but also give much better braking performance when wet. For that reason a damaged steel rim should preferably be replaced by an aluminum version.

The kind of damage done to a rim consists of bending the thing out of shape – either a small dent or nick, or a bigger bend, resulting in wheel wobble – and (especially on very light rims and those which are not reinforced at the spoke holes) cracking at the spoke

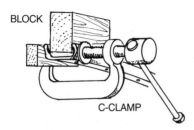

BLOCK

C-CLAMP

holes. The large gentle bend can usually be straightened by means of spoke tension corrections, as described under *Wheel Truing* below. The other kinds of damage usually require rim replacement.

Select a rim that matches the kind of tire you intend to use, both as regards nominal size and as regards width. A wide cross section tire fits best on a relatively wide rim; a narrow rim can only be used with light narrow tires with very flexible sidewalls; foldable tires require narrow rims with hook edges pointing in. A temporary rim repair may be acceptable, being the only thing to keep you on the road until you can replace the rim, if a small sharp dent – usually the result of hitting a sharp object at speed with a tire that's not inflated adequately – is your problem. To minimize the effect the dent has on braking or the way the tire is seated, remove the tire and bend the rim back, following the illustration.

The Spokes
The illustration shows the two basic types of spokes: plain gauge (the same thickness along its entire length) and butted (thicker at the ends than in the center section). In addition, spokes are available in several thicknesses

(called gauges), a higher gauge number indicating a thinner spoke. Note how the length of the spoke is determined: from the threaded end to the inside of the bend at the head. The length is usually quoted in mm. Different spoke lengths are required for different wheel sizes, rim types, hub flange types and spoking patterns – there are just too many variables to systematically keep track of: ask at the bike shop if you're in doubt. Spokes are tightened (and with them the entire wheel) by turning in the nipples with which they are held to the rim. To establish which way the nipple should be turned, refer to the illustration.

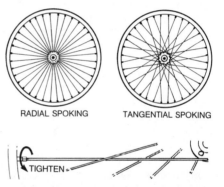

RADIAL SPOKING   TANGENTIAL SPOKING

TIGHTEN

Spokes are usually installed tangentially, which – as opposed to radial spoking – allows the transmission of torque. Since torque is only of concern in a driven (rear) wheel or in a wheel with a hub brake, most front wheels could be spoked radially with impunity. However, it has become customary to standardize on spoking patterns. I generally recommend four-cross spoking, whereby each spoke crosses four other spokes on the same hub

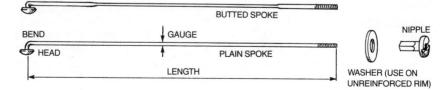

BUTTED SPOKE
BEND · GAUGE
HEAD · PLAIN SPOKE
LENGTH · NIPPLE · WASHER (USE ON UNREINFORCED RIM)

flange. This is the only true tangential pattern, which gives the strongest wheel that is also adequately rigid against lateral and radial deformation. However, on a high flange hub three-cross spoking is the best that can be used, due to interference between spokes at the heads. All this applies to wheels with the usual number of 36 spokes (i.e. 18 spokes on each side); wheels with more spokes (e.g. tandem wheels) should have more crosses.

Before tackling any spoke related job, I suggest you take a close look at the wheel as it is presently spoked, and at the various drawings which accompany these instructions. Some wheels have been installed incorrectly (or were botched before), so it is good to know how the wheel should look from the drawings. Try to visually separate just the spokes that run from one side of one flange of the wheel, then see how they relate to the spokes that lie on the other side of the same flange, and finally see how the spokes from the two flanges fill up the entire rim. The pattern repeats itself every fourth spoke. When checking to see how it all fits together, start by looking either side of the spoke hole: there the two spokes on either side run more or less parallel, one to the near-side hub flange, the other one to the far-side flange. Also note how the spoke holes in the rim are off-set to the side corresponding to this pattern (technically this is not much help, but it reduces the chances of mixing up the pattern while installing the spokes).

Replace Identical Rim

If the rim will be replaced with one of identical design and size, keeping hub and spokes unchanged, this is the easiest method for an inexperienced person. The wheel must be taken out of the bike, and tire, tube and rim tape removed from the rim.

Tools and equipment
☐ spoke wrench (nippel spanner in Britain)
☐ medium size screwdriver
☐ lubricant (e.g. vaseline)
☐ rag

Procedure
1. Place the new rim on top of the old one, lining up the valve holes; verify whether indeed the two rims are similar enough to be called 'identical' – especially the depth of the rim and the way the spoke holes are off-set either side of the centerline must be the same (i.e. both off-set the same direction in the same location). If the rims are not identical, proceed to the instruction *Spoking the Wheel,* below.
2. Tape the new rim to the old one in at least three points between spoke holes, so that they are completely lined up, with the valve holes in the same location.

LINE UP VALVE HOLES

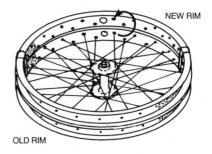

NEW RIM

OLD RIM

3. Loosen the nipples one by one, lubricate the spoke end and fasten it in the same location in the new rim, working around the wheel; leave a little more spoke thread exposed than before to allow subsequent tightening.
4. When all the spokes are installed, proceed to the adjusting and straightening procedure, point 13 under *Spoking the Wheel,* below.

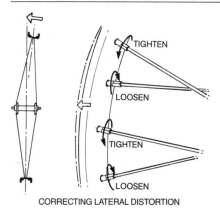

CORRECTING LATERAL DISTORTION

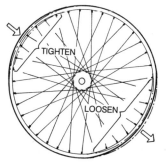

CORRECTING RADIAL DISTORTION

Wheel Truing

Sometimes the wheel gets out of shape, so that it seems to wobble either sideways or up and down as it is rotated. It is also possible that the entire wheel is off-center, so that the two wheels don't track properly, even though the frame and the fork are perfectly straight. Each of these problems is similarly corrected by means of tightening and loosening certain spokes. As long as the problem is not too dramatic, it can usually be solved without removing the tire, although that does make the work easier. The wheel must be installed in the bike.

Tools and equipment
☐ spoke wrench (in an emergency, you may use a small crescent wrench instead)
☐ chalk or other marking material (though it can be done without, at a pinch)

Procedure
1. Rotate the wheel slowly and observe how the position of the rim

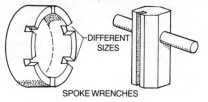

DIFFERENT SIZES

SPOKE WRENCHES

changes relative to a fixed reference point, such as the stays or a rim brake. Determine this way where it has to be moved further one way or the other (left, right, up, down) or, if it is not centered, mount the wheel the other way round to determine how much it is off-set, and in which direction.

2. Tighten and loosen individual spokes in the affected area, as shown in the illustrations. For radial out-of-roundness, tighten all the spokes in the high spot or loosen those in the low spot (several turns at the worst point, decreasing to perhaps only half a turn near the ends), then loosen or tighten all the other spokes a quarter turn at a time as appropriate, until all spokes have the same tension and the wheel is round.

3. For lateral deflections (the more typical problem, often resulting from a single broken spoke), first replace any missing spokes. Loosen the spokes on the side towards which the rim is off-set locally (again, more in the middle, e.g. a whole turn, less towards the end, e.g. a quarter of a turn) and tighten the spokes that run to the opposite hub flange by similar amounts. Repeat until the wheel is perfectly true. If the tension of the spokes becomes very high in places, while the wheel remains bent, loosen all spokes one turn, then start again.

FRONT
(SYMMETRIC)

REAR
(DISHED)

REAR
(SYMMETRIC)

Replace Individual Spoke

Replace missing spokes as soon as possible. Preferably, both spoke and nipple should be replaced (locally remove the tire, the tube and the rim tape to get access to the nipple in the rim). Measure the spoke length very carefully, adding 2–3 mm ($\frac{3}{32}$ in) to the measured length from the outside edge of the spoke hole in the hub flange to the inside of the rim. Especially if you reuse the old nipple, choose a spoke of the same thickness as the old one.

4. For a wheel that is off-center, loosen all the spokes that run to the side where the rim is too far from the centerline, and tighten all spokes on the other side by an equal amount – perhaps one half turn at a time – until the wheel is centered. After you have made this correction, check and, if necessary, correct for radial and lateral alignment in accordance with points 2 and 3 above.

Note: It is preferable to check each wheel for centering with a special tool (see Chapter 13) or by the method illustrated below, requiring some equally high blocks and a long straightedge. The easiest and surest way to give you the equivalent of a long, perfect straightedge is to make a bow, using a long thin flexible rod and some thin string. Measure and compare the two sides of the wheel in at least two different locations around the wheel.

The spokes that are most likely to break are exactly those that are least accessible, namely those on the RH side of the rear wheel, where they are covered by the freewheel or the sprocket. Remove the freewheel or sprocket (see Chapter 6) in that case. Apply a little lubricant at the screw thread, which will make subsequent replacement and adjustments easier. Wind the spoke in the same way as another spoke on the same side of the same hub flange – remember: the spoke pattern is repeated every fourth spoke on the rim, which corresponds to every second spoke on the same hub flange. After you have inserted and tightened the new spoke, check to make sure the end does not protrude beyond the nipple inside the rim, where it could damage the tube (file off if necessary), and cover the area with rim tape before installing the tire. Finally, check and, if necessary, correct for roundness in accordance with the instructions in the preceding description *Wheel Truing.*

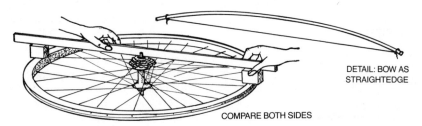

DETAIL: BOW AS STRAIGHTEDGE

COMPARE BOTH SIDES

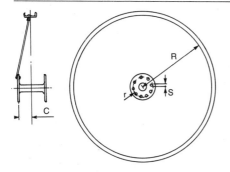

Wheel Building

This is the biggest wheel project, and it is one I only recommend you to do if you are really ambitious: a professional can do it so much faster that it is probably worth the money to have him do it. But it's wonderful therapy, and becomes easier as you do it more often. Before you start, take a very close look at the old wheel (or an other similar wheel) and the various descriptions and drawings in this chapter that show spoking details – try to *understand* what's going on before you start.

Make sure you get the right spoke length – ask at the bike shop, telling them which hub and which rim you will be combining and which spoking pattern (radial, one-, two-, three-, four-cross) you'll be using, and how many spokes will be used. Most wheels are built with 36 spokes, and for structural reasons I recommend using a four-cross pattern with low flange hubs (you'll be restricted to a maximum of three-cross when using high-flange hubs). On an off-set rear wheel (especially one used with a six-speed or seven-speed freewheel block) the spokes on the RH side should be about 3 mm (⅛ in) shorter than those on the LH side; so, if you can't find the optimum spoke size, deviate a little on the low side for the spokes on the RH side, a little on the high side for the LH spokes. If you are up to trigonometric calculations (or rather, if your hand-held calculator is),you may use the following formula to calculate the spoke length (all dimensions in mm).

Spoke length = $\sqrt{A + B + C} - 0.5\,S$

where: A = r sin (T)

B = R − r cos (T)

C = off-set from outside hub flange to center of wheel (on front wheel, that's one half of total hub width, on rear wheel it's different on both sides)

r = ½ effective hub diameter

R = ½ effective rim diameter

T = 360 X/N

X = number of spoke crossings

N = number of spokes per hub flange (usually: one half total number of spokes)

S = spoke hole diameter in hub flange

You will be excused if you're scared off by this formula, but it's there for whoever needs it. Alternatively, here's a method of determining relatively painlessly whether you are using the correct spoke length, based on the principle that any plane is determined by three points.

Spoke Length Check

Use this method whenever you are not absolutely sure whether you have the correct spoke length. If the spoke length is found to be correct, you may continue spoking the entire wheel by the pattern thus established. You'll need only six spokes – check whether they are all equally long first: hold them upright on the table, screwed ends down, and compare the height of the heads.

Tools and equipment
☐ spoke wrench
☐ medium screwdriver
☐ lubricant (e.g. vaseline)
☐ rag

Procedure

1. Take six spokes and nipples; lubricate the spoke ends and wipe off.

2. Hold the hub upright in front of you. On the upper hub flange, select three holes that are equally spaced (every sixth in the case of a 36-hole hub, which has 18 holes per flange; if the hub has more or less than 36 holes, you may not be able to space completely equally – just make sure the spokes are spaced as equally as possible, with an *odd number* of empty spoke holes in the flange between the spokes). If the hub has holes that are alternately countersunk ('beveled'), select holes that are beveled on the *inside.* Put a spoke through each of these holes from the outside through to the inside.

3. Inspect the spoke holes in the rim: take the hole next to the valve hole that is off-set up (on most rims sold in the US that is the first hole going counterclockwise, but it may also be the first one going clockwise, especially on Italian rims). Attach one of the three spokes with the nipple in this hole. Mark it with adhesive tape – we'll call it *spoke 1* for later reference when completing the spoking pattern.

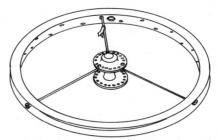

4. Count out the same number of holes that are off-set upward as there are vacant holes in the hub, going the same direction (clockwise or counterclockwise). Place the other two spokes in the corresponding holes determined this way. Now the spokes in the upper hub flange should be connected to similarly spaced holes that are off-set upward in the rim – correct if necessary.

5. Turn the wheel over, so that the hub flange without spokes faces up.

6. Visually line up the two hub flanges, noting how the holes in the near flange are positioned between the holes in the far flange. I'll call this off-set from one hole in the one flange to the nearest hole in the other flange a 'half space', while I'll call the space between consecutive holes in the same flange a (whole) space.

Table 9-I – Spoke hole spacing in hub for neighboring spokes in rim

No. of spokes in wheel	1-cross angle	spaces	2-cross angle	spaces	3-cross angle	spaces	4-cross angle	spaces	5-cross angle	spaces
24	75°	2½	135°	4½	–	–	–	–	–	–
28	64.3°	2½	115.7°	4½	167.1°	6½	–	–	–	–
32	56.3°	2½	101.3°	4½	146.3°	6½	–	–	–	–
36	50°	2½	90°	4½	130°	6½	170°	8½	–	–
40	45°	2½	81°	4½	117°	6½	153°	8½	–	–
44	40.9°	2½	73.6°	4½	106.4°	6½	139.1°	8½	171.8°	10½
48	37.5°	2½	67.5°	4½	97.5°	6½	127.5°	8½	157.5°	10½

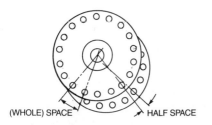

(WHOLE) SPACE   HALF SPACE

7. To find the location for the first spoke inserted on the flange that is on top now, read off the number of spaces from the table, as a function of the number of spokes and the number of spoke crossings required (e.g. 8½ for a four-cross pattern with 36 spokes). Count out the appropriate number of spaces from the hole where spoke 1 (marked with tape) is located in the direction of the valve hole (i.e. going counterclockwise if the valve hole is counterclockwise from the spoke). In the hub flange hole thus established, insert a spoke from the outside to the inside, and attach this spoke to the free spoke hole in the rim immediately adjacent to the valve hole.

8. Count out the same number of spoke holes in the hub on either side of this spoke as you count between corresponding spokes on the lower flange either side of spoke 1, inserting the two remaining spokes there, again from the outside to the inside.

9. Attach these spokes to the rim in the holes that are in the same relative position to each other as the two spokes on either side of the valve hole.

10. Stop to check whether you've got something that looks like the illus-

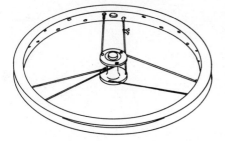

tration, and – if not – where you went wrong. Correct anything that is amiss.

11. Tighten the six spokes gradually until the wheel is reasonably tight and centered (front wheel) or appropriately off-set (dished rear wheel) as required. If significant thread is exposed under the nipple (more than 1 thread), choose a longer spoke; if any part of the spoke protrudes beyond the nipple inside the rim, choose a shorter spoke – and start all over again. If the spoke length is correct, continue building the wheel more or less as described in the following procedure *Spoking the Wheel,* starting at point 4.

Note: If you are building a radially spoked (front) wheel, insert all spokes from the inside to the outside, so they all lie on the outside of the hub flanges.

Spoking the Wheel

This instruction is based on the assumption that you have determined the correct spoke length. If you're not sure, first carry out the check described above under *Spoke Length Check,* after which you'll be well on your way and can pick up the instructions starting at point 4. If you're rebuilding a wheel using an old hub or an old rim (or both), first cut away all the old spokes and remove them. If you're re-using the spokes and the hub, follow the earlier instruction *Replace Identical Rim.*

Tools and equipment
☐ spoke wrench
☐ medium size screwdriver
☐ lubricant (e.g. vaseline)
☐ rag

Procedure
1. Check whether all the spokes have the same length: take them all in your hand, push them end-down on the table, and compare the heights of the heads. Lubricate the threaded ends and wipe off excess lubricant.

2. Take nine spokes (assuming a 36-spoke wheel – more or less for other wheels), and put one through every second hole in one of the hub flanges from the outside to the inside. If holes are alternately countersunk on the inside and the outside of the hub flange, select those holes that are countersunk on the inside.

3. Putting the hub in front of you, held vertically with the batch of spokes stuck through the upper flange, find the spoke hole in the hub that's immediately next to the valve hole and is off-set upward. Take one spoke and attach it with the nipple to that hole; mark this spoke (e.g. with tape) we'll call it *spoke 1*. Screw on the nipple about five turns.

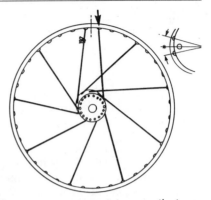

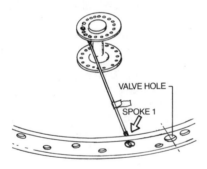

VALVE HOLE

SPOKE 1

4. Similarly attach the other spokes so far installed in the hub into every fourth hole in the rim. If you followed the instruction *Spoke Length Check* above, just put in the remaining spokes – you already have three of them.

5. Check to make sure all these spokes are attached to spoke holes that are off-set upward in the rim, and that three free spoke holes remain between each pair of consecutive spokes in the rim, one free hole in the hub.

6. Turn the wheel over and establish whether the remaining free hole immediately next to the valve hole is oriented clockwise or counterclockwise. Select the spoke holes in the

flange now nearest to you that are each off-set half a space from the spokes already installed on the far flange in that same direction. Insert the next set of nine (or whatever is the appropriate number) spokes in these holes, leaving a free hole between each set of consecutive spokes.

7. Locate spoke 1 (the one on the far flange next to the valve hole) and count out the appropriate number of spaces to determine where the next spoke is, which you'll attach in the free spoke hole on the other side of the valve hole (refer to Table 9.I) counting clockwise if the free spoke hole is also clockwise from the valve hole, counterclockwise if the free hole is counterclockwise from the valve hole. If you followed the instruction *Spoke Length Check* this has already been determined – just install the missing spokes.

8. Attach the remaining spokes so far inserted in the hub into every fourth spoke hole in the rim.

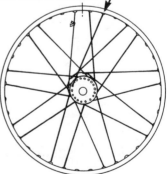

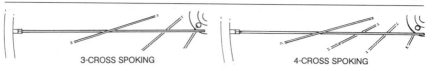

3-CROSS SPOKING   4-CROSS SPOKING

9. You should now have sets of two spokes, each set separated by two free holes in the rim and by one free hole in the hub flanges. Make any corrections that may be required.

10. Insert the next batch of spokes from the inside to the outside in one of the hub flanges.

11. Take any one of these spokes and 'lace' it to cross the chosen number of spokes on the same hub flange for the crossing pattern selected, always crossing under the last one. If you're building a four-cross wheel that will be over the first, over the second, over the third and then forced under the fourth. Attach this spoke in the next free hole in the rim that's offset in the corresponding direction. If it doesn't fit, you either have the wrong spoke length for the pattern selected, have tightened the other spokes too much (rarely the case), or you made a mistake somewhere along the line – check and restart if necessary.

12. Do the same with the last batch of spokes, inserting them in the free holes in the other hub flange from the inside to the outside, making the right crossings; then install them in the remaining spoke holes in the rim.

13. You now have a complete, but loosely spoked, wheel. Once more check to make sure the patten is correct as you intended, then start tightening the spoke nipples progressively, working around several times, first using the screwdriver, then – when the nipples begin to get tighter – with the spoke wrench. Don't tighten too much though: it should remain easy to turn the nipples with the spoke wrench.

14. Check whether the wheel is correctly centered between the locknuts at the wheel axle, as outlined in the description *Wheel Truing* above under point 4 and the subsequent note.

15. Install the wheel in the bike, which should be hung up off the ground by saddle and handlebars or placed upside-down (taking care to support it at the handlebars so nothing gets damaged), and make the same kind of corrections as outlined under *Wheel Truing* above, until the wheel is perfectly round and has no lateral deflection.

16. Proceed to tighten the spokes all around equally. Unless you're an experienced piano-tuner, it's hard to explain in writing how tight is right. Just compare with another good wheel (ask in the bike shop) to develop a feel for the right tension. Tension is checked by pushing spokes together in crossed pairs at a point between the rim and the last cross. On an offset rear wheel, the RH spokes (chain side) should be considerably tighter than those on the other side. All the spokes on the same side of a wheel must be equally tight.

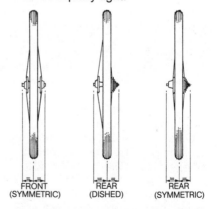

FRONT   REAR   REAR
(SYMMETRIC)   (DISHED)   (SYMMETRIC)

17. Now take spokes together in sets of four – two nearby sets of crossed spokes on each side of the wheel –

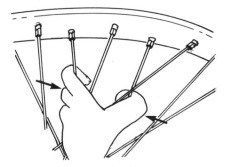

at the point of their last crossing and squeeze them together quite forcefully. This will bend the spokes into their final shape and release all sorts of built-up stresses, resulting in some disturbing sounds. Don't be perturbed – if you don't do this now it will happen while you're riding the bike, when it's too late to make the required corrections.

18. After this stress-relieving operation, check the wheel for roundness and tightness once more – you will probably have to tighten several spokes a little more, since they have straightened and some will have partly 'unwound' from their nipples.

19. After perhaps 40 km (25 miles) of cycling, check and true the wheel once more. It's a lot of work, but think of the satisfaction.

Note: A radially spoked wheel (front wheel only) is simpler, since all spokes are then inserted from the inside to the outside, finishing up on the outside of the hub flanges of the finished wheel.

The Tires

Two different categories of tires are in use for bicycles: the wired-on tire, consisting of separate cover and inner tube, and the tubular tire (referred to as tub in Britain, sew-up in the US). The latter type is primarily used in bicycle racing; the former is the more universally used. Tire and rim must be matched: narrow sprint rims are used to mount tubular tires. Many different

sizes (both as regards diameter and as regards width) of matching Endrick type rims and wired-on tires are available for different bike types and purposes.

In general, wider and heavier tires are used for poorer road surfaces. The most common sizes are 27 x 1¼ in (nominally – in reality most models now popular are considerably narrower) and 700 C for ten-speed bicycles, mounted on rims of 630 mm and 622 mm tire seat diameter, respectively. Other popular sizes are 26 x 2.125 or 26 x 1.75, as used for mountain bikes and many American utility bikes, mounted on 559 mm tire seat diameter rims. British 26-in tires are much narrower and are not interchangeable with the American size; they are mounted on rims with a tire seat diameter of 584 mm. French 650 B tires are also somewhat similar in size to 26-in tires, but again narrower (though still thicker than the British 26-in models) and are mounted on rims with a tire seat diameter of 671 mm.

This is about as far as I can go on the subject of tire sizing in what must primarily remain a repair manual. In the remaining sections of this chapter I shall cover the various repair and replacement jobs associated with tires, tubes and tubular tires.

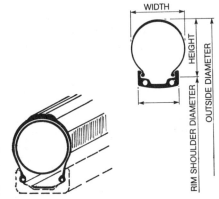

Repair Regular (i.e. Wired-on) Tire

This is probably the first and most frequent repair job on the bicycle you'll encounter. It is much easier and quicker to solve than most cyclists presume, so this repair can easily be handled *en-route.* But it pays to practice at home – when I give bike repair courses, I pierce the participants' tires with a pin, which will force them to do this job; almost all report later that they're grateful for it, since they would not otherwise have had the confidence to tackle the job away from home. Proceed as follows, and don't be scared off by the length of the description: it can be done very quickly, although a lot of words are needed to describe the work.

Tools and equipment
□ tire patch kit (including adhesive patches, rubber solution, sandpaper, talcum powder)
□ three tire irons (called tyre levers in Britain)
□ pump
□ any tools required to remove the wheel

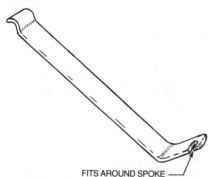

FITS AROUND SPOKE

Procedure
1. Except in the case of a wheel on a bike with a hub brake or roller-lever brake (where it would be more trouble than it's worth), remove the wheel from the bike, as described elsewhere in this chapter. If the wheel stays in the bike, put the bike upside-down,

Schraeder   Presta   Woods (Dunlop)

UNSCREW BEFORE INFLATING

taking the usual precautions to protect whatever is mounted on the handlebars.

2. Check the valve: try to pump up and listen whether air is escaping there; if it is, see whether tightening the valve mechanism will do the trick. This is rarely the case, but it's worth trying.

3. Check the circumference of the tire cover for signs of damage, such as pinched or split spots or embedded sharp objects. Remove any embedded object and mark the location somehow: the leak will probably be there, so that's where you'll look first, once you have taken the tire off the wheel.

4. Let out any remaining air at the valve (Presta valve: unscrew and push in; Schraeder valve: push the internal pin in; Woods valve: disassemble). Remove any locknut that may be installed on the valve body.

5. Pushing the near side of the tire into the deepest part of the rim, work around the tire with both hands in opposite directions to create maximum 'slack' at the top of the wheel. At that point install one tire iron with the tip of the longer leg tucked under the tire bead and the shorter leg with its cut-out hooked over the nearest spoke.

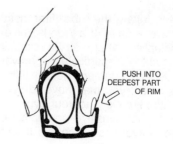

PUSH INTO DEEPEST PART OF RIM

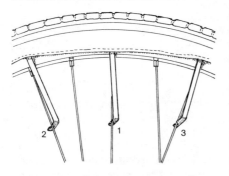

6. About 4–5 inches to the right, push in a second tire iron and secure it the same way; 4–5 inches the other direction you do the same with the third tire iron. As you lift the tire bead over the edge of the rim, the middle tire iron will come loose–use it as a fourth, if needed.

7. Put the tips of your fingers under the tire bead (nails against the side of the rim) and pull the near side of the tire off over the edge of the rim over its entire length.

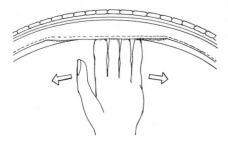

8. Carefully pull the tube out, and work the valve out of its hole in the rim from under the tire cover. Try to remember where you suspected damage.

9. Inflate the tube (first install the valve in case of a Woods valve) and establish where air is escaping – watching in particular wherever you suspected damage before. If the hole is small, you may have to pass the entire tire close to your eye, which is the most sensitive perceptive organ you have when it comes to noticing faint air streams. If you don't even find it this way, dip the tire in a water bath – a small section at a time, watching for escaping air bubbles. Sometimes there are several holes: make sure you find them all. Mark each hole with e.g. a ball point pen, drawing a big circle (bigger than the patch you'll use) centered around it. Make sure the tire is dry before proceeding.

10. Clean and roughen the area around the hole with sandpaper; wipe off, then lightly spread rubber solution on an area slightly bigger than the patch. If it is a tear or a big hole, choose a bigger patch, and be careful not to enlarge it any further. Allow the rubber solution to dry about 3–4 minutes, so it's not tacky any more.

11. Take the aluminum foil, cloth or plastic backing off the adhesive side of the patch; then firmly place the patch exactly in the right position over the hole, and contacting the tire only where it was coated with rubber solution. Do not try to move it: once it's on, it should stay; or, if it's not in the right position, remove it immediately and start all over again with a new patch at point 10. Apply firm pressure briefly, then stretch tire and patch, holding both together, in several directions, until you're sure the patch is on properly. Should the patch lift off anywhere, it must be removed and you'll have to start all over again at point 10 above. Inflate the tube.

12. Inspect the inside of the tire cover; remove anything that might damage the tube. Repair any tears or holes that cut through the tire cover on the inside with a patch made of a piece of an old tubular tire (get a discarded one at a bike shop) with rubber solution on the patch and the tire carcass, or use handlebar tape at a pinch. Cuts in the rubber of the tire cover can be repaired with anaerobic cyanacrilate adhesive ('magic glue' or some such name – it used to be advertised with a picture

that showed a car hanging off something held with one drop of this adhesive). Just be careful when using this
kind of adhesive: it will permanently
and irreparably stick your fingers
together just as effectively. Open up
the cut, which must be clean, insert
one drop of adhesive, then push the
tire in such a way that the cut is closed
– hold one minute, and you're in business. A tire that is badly worn or damaged must of course be replaced; the
same goes for a tube that is severely
damaged (burst or torn), or that has
become porous, i.e. gradually loses
air even if no puncture can be found.

13. Inspect the rim tape that should
cover all the spoke nipples inside the
rim; if you find any spokes protruding
from the nipples, file them flush first.

14. If the tube held air while you
were doing the work described in
points 12 and 13, sprinkle talcum
powder over the area around the
patch, let out most air again (all air in
case you have a Woods type valve,
which must be disassembled). Install
the valve in the valve hole in the rim,
and work the tube under the tire cover
(Woods valve: assemble first and inflate the tube slightly).

15. Starting opposite the valve, pull
the bead of the tire over the edge of
the rim, working in both directions
simultaneously with your bare hands
(don't use tire irons or any other tools,

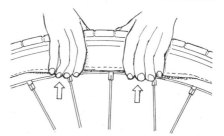

since you would probably pinch the
tube). Work the bead of the tire into
the deepest part of the rim (you may
have to let some more air escape to
achieve that). Continue until you are
about six inches either side of the
valve and you notice the going gets
tougher. The valve should be near the
top of the wheel before proceeding,
the uninstalled side of the tire away
from you.

16. Push the valve up inside the rim
until only about half its length projects.
Take a deep breath, grab the tire with
both hands at the bottom; forcefully
push the tire wall on the uninstalled
side into the deeper center of the rim,
working it in as you 'sweep' the two
semi-circles until your hands meet
near the valve. This action should
have provided enough slack in the tire
section that remains outside the rim
to allow you to force it over the edge.
In very difficult cases (when tire and
rim are a poor match), it may be necessary to remove the tire again and
to apply soap to both the tire bead and
the edge and the inside of the rim –
the soap will reduce friction enough to
get any tire on that is not definitely the
wrong size. If you can't do it as described, the only safe tool to use is the
one illustrated.

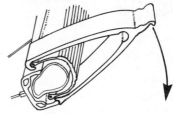

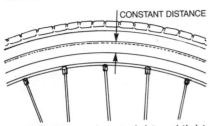

CONSTANT DISTANCE

17. Pull the valve straight and tighten up the locknut; then inflate just a little more.

18. 'Kneed' the sides of the tire to assure the tube is not caught (pinched) anywhere under the tire bead. The tire should be seated concentrically, which you can verify by checking the distance between the edge of the rim and the concentric ridge on the tire sidewall – make any corrections that may be required.

19. Inflate the tire to its proper pressure – at least as high as the rating printed on the side of the tire. I suggest you buy a tire pressure gauge for the specific kind of valve used on the bike (available for Presta and Schraeder valves), unless you have calibrated your thumb to perceive what is the correct pressure. Most people tend to inflate insufficiently – and insufficient pressure is the cause of most punctures.

20. Install the wheel in the bike and check to make sure the wheel is free to turn and any adjustments disturbed are corrected.

PRESSURE GAUGE

Replace Tire or Tube

Worn or damaged tires and defective tubes should be replaced. Buy the type and size to match your rim and your riding style. Remove the old tire and the tube as described in steps 1

and 4–8 in the preceding instruction, then also pull the other tire bead over the edge of the rim (if it's the tire cover that has to be replaced). Check to make sure no spokes are protruding and that the rim tape is intact, or replace it, using adhesive cloth tape if the rim is of the double bottom or box section design, in which the nipples are recessed very deeply, butyl (stretchy) rim tape in all other cases. When installing, first put on one tire bead, then the tube, and finally the other tire bead, following points 14–20 in the repair instruction immediately preceding.

Replace Valve

Although most people will replace a tube if it is damaged near the valve or if the valve itself is leaking, it is possible to make a repair at this point, providing the valve is not vulcanized or moulded together with the tube, but screwed on. For that purpose, keep a good valve of a discarded tube to use as a spare. Remove the defective valve, then mend the hole with a big patch as though it were a regular puncture. Put a big patch on the tube in some other suitable location for the valve; carefully cut a small hole in the middle, going through the patch and the tube. Work the base of the valve through this hole, and clamp down the valve with the washer and the small hexagonal locknut that held the valve in place on the original tube. Inflate and check – correct if necessary.

FILE BASE AND WASHER AS SHOWN
FOR NARROW RIM

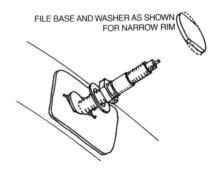

Repair Tubular Tire

Patching a tubular tire is a work of love – if you have neither the patience to do it, nor the money to have someone else do it or to replace each punctured tubular tire, you'd be better off installing wired-on tires (and the matching rims). Even if you don't do the repair yourself, you will have to know how to remove and install tubular tires – two instructions that follow this one. The repair instruction is based on the assumption that the tire has been removed from the bike: it's a job to do at home.

Tools and equipment
☐ special tubular tire patch kit (comprising patches, rubber solution, sandpaper, twine, needle, thimble, and talcum powder (often in the form of a stick which you scrape to obtain powder)
☐ sharp knife
☐ pump

Procedure
1. Inflate the tire to find out where the hole is. Listen or, if you don't hear escaping air, pass the entire tire surface closely past your eyes, which are very sensitive to this kind of thing; if this doesn't work either, submerge the tire in water, a section at a time, watching for escaping air bubbles. Mark the location of the leak.

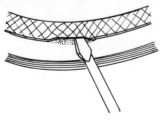

2. Over an area about 4–5 inches either side of the leak, remove the backing tape, using a thin object.

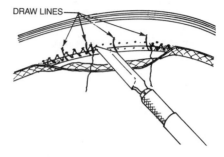

3. Draw a ball-point line every half inch across the seam in the tire, then cut away the stitching over a length of about 6 inches, centered about the leak. Remove the loose remains of the stitching.
4. Dig the tube out from under the backing strip; repair the puncture as described for a regular puncture in *Repair Regular (i.e. Wired-on) Tire,* points 9–12 and 14 above.
5. Put the tube back in the cover, and pull the backing tape and the cover itself together, lining up the lines you had drawn before.
6. Holding back the tube so it will not get damaged, carefully sew together the seam, not pulling it so tight that it will not lie flat. Work the ends of the twine back under the stitching to prevent it from unraveling.

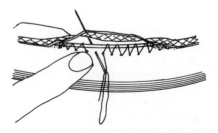

7. Using the regular rubber solution on the tire cover and the cover tape, glue the tape back into place.

Note: Keep spare tires in a cool dry place, preferably inflated somewhat, and best of all installed around a spare rim. Just don't forget to pack a spare when you are out riding; release it from its tightly folded position for proper storage when you get home.

Remove Tubular Tire

To remove the tire when you have a puncture, first remove the wheel from the bike. Starting opposite the valve, roll off the tire with the palms of both hands, working around the tire in both directions; finally, remove the valve from the rim. When folding up the tire, take care to do it in such a way that the adhesive backing does not stick together.

Install Tubular Tire

When you have a puncture on the way, it is perfectly satisfactory to simply install the spare on the still tacky rim, merely taking care not to corner so wildly that the thing might come off. For a permanent installation, proceed as follows.

Tools and equipment
☐ either: tube of tire adhesive, or: double-sided adhesive tire-mounting tape (the latter is easier to use; it is, however, hard to get in parts of the US, though readily available elsewhere)
☐ acetone or other solvent
☐ pump

Procedure
1. Clean off the old adhesive with acetone or remove the old adhesive tape.
2. When using adhesive compound: spread an even layer on the entire rim bed, subsequently cleaning your hands either with acetone or (preferably) with waterless hand cleaner.
3. When using adhesive tape: wrap the tape around the rim tightly, starting just before the valve hole and ending just after (i.e. overlapping at the valve hole), centering the tape carefully. Push it down with a firm rounded object like the handle of a screwdriver. Cut a hole for the valve, then remove the paper backing strip, also from the overlapped part.
4. Slightly moisten the adhesive rim bed, so the tire does not adhere fully before it is properly positioned. Place a strip of paper, about two inches wide, opposite the valve hole; this will give you a good place to start removal of the tire when it has to be replaced later.
5. Inflate the tire somewhat. If you're installing a brand new tire, first stretch it, holding it down with your feet, as you pull the opposite end up forcefully with your hands.

6. Insert the valve, then place the tire on the rim, centering it properly as you work all around the rim (compare the concentricity of the sidewall).

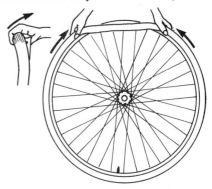

7. Inflate to the final pressure, then check and correct concentricity once more. Remove any spilled adhesive and tear off the ends of the paper strip opposite the valve. Wait at least overnight before using the wheel, so the adhesive will be cured.

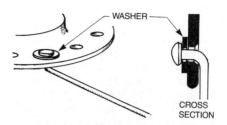

Tandem Wheels

Tandem riders seem to have never ending wheel problems. Especially on the rear wheel spoke breakage can be a perennial headache. One reason is that the stoker often is not adequately aware of the condition of the road, and leaves his full weight resting on the wheel when riding over a ridge or through a pothole. Use the strongest rims, the strongest hubs and the strongest spokes (for which you may have to drill out the holes in the hubs), spoked in a four-cross pattern (if you use 36 spokes – even better is to use wheels with more spokes and crossing them as many times as possible).

Mount strong tires of significant cross section, and keep them inflated to the highest pressure allowed. Keep the wheels well trued and the spoke tension high and equal. Avoid six- and seven-speed freewheels, since that dishes the wheel too far for the heavy load of tandem riding. If the spokes seem to be somewhat loose at the hub – i.e. if the hub flange seems too narrow to fill the entire bend of the spoke head – you can usually reduce the chances of spoke breakage by installing 3 mm (⅛ in) ID washers under the spoke heads, as shown in the illustration.

10
The Brakes

Except on simple utility bikes and a few specialty machines, hand-operated rim brakes are used almost universally these days. Consequently, the greater part of this chapter will be devoted to their maintenance, while the care of the various special brakes will be described briefly towards the end of the chapter. It is no coincidence that the rim brake of modern design has become so widely used: it is without a doubt the most effective device for stopping a bicycle under most conditions. Other brakes do have limited advantages for certain uses, but the modern rim brake is the most universally effective brake.

Four basically different types of rim brakes are in use – not considering for a moment the pull-rod operated stirrup or roller-lever brake, which is still in use on heavy utility bikes in Britain. The four basic types are depicted here. All are operated by means of handles via Bowden cables, and act by pushing brake shoes together against the sides of the rim simultaneously from both sides. Most common is the sidepull brake, on which the brake arms pivot around a common mounting bolt. The centerpull brake has separate pivots mounted on a common connecting yoke. The cantilever brake – most popular on off-road

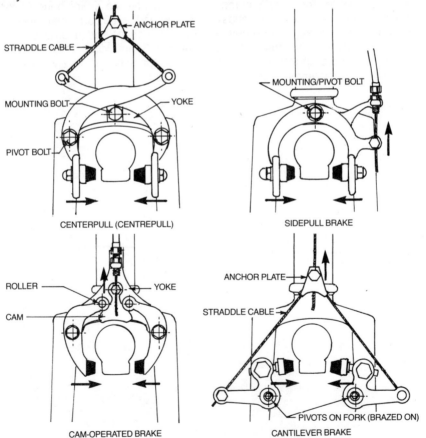

CENTERPULL (CENTREPULL)

SIDEPULL BRAKE

CAM-OPERATED BRAKE

CANTILEVER BRAKE

bicycles and tandems – is similar to the centerpull brake, except that here the pivots are each mounted on a brazed-on attachment, rather than on a separate yoke. The cam-operated design is a centerpull variant on which the brake arms are operated via a cam-shaped plate, which pushes the rollers on the brake arms apart as it is pulled up.

2 CM MINIMUM

Rim Brake Maintenance

All rim brakes are similarly operated, and it is this operating mechanism with its Bowden cables that requires most maintenance. They must be adjusted from time to time, to compensate for brake block wear. The other most common maintenance jobs, which are similar for all types, are brake block replacement, checking the attachments, lubricating the cables and – only too often forgotten – cleaning the sides of the rims upon which the brake blocks operate.

Rim Brake Adjustment

To check whether a rim brake is operating optimally, carry out the following check and subsequent adjustment procedure. But first make sure the brake is attached properly, the brake cable is firmly mounted and free to move, and the rim is dry and clean. If necessary, clean off greasy dirt and brake block material traces with solvent. It may also help to lubricate the cable at the points where you see the inner cable disappear into the outer cable, both at the lever (pull the lever for access to this point) and where the outer cable is anchored at the adjustment mechanism. Another cause for poor braking may be a rim that is out of true, i.e. one that seems to wobble sideways as the wheel is turned (see the instructions in Chapter 9 for correction). Finally, the brake pads must lie on the rim over their entire width and length when the brake is applied.

Checking procedure

1. The front brake is checked by riding the bike at walking speed and then pulling the appropriate brake handle fully, keeping the hand on the other lever ready to apply it, too. The front brake must retard the bike enough to start the rear wheel's lifting off the ground. As you feel this happening, you should let go of the front brake. This braking effect should be achieved with some distance left between the brake lever and the handlebars – I'd say about ¾ in.

2. The rear brake is checked by similarly riding at walking speed and then pulling the appropriate lever. The rear brake must work adequately firmly to block the wheel and make the tire skid. Let go of the brake again as soon as the wheel begins to skid, to regain control.

Adjusting procedure

1. Find the barrel adjuster for the brake to be adjusted: on most cantilever and centerpull brakes at the point where the outer cable ends on the frame, on sidepull brakes directly on the brake arm where the outer cable ends.

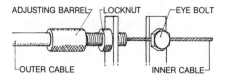

ADJUSTING BARREL ┐ ┌LOCKNUT   ┌EYE BOLT

└OUTER CABLE   INNER CABLE┘

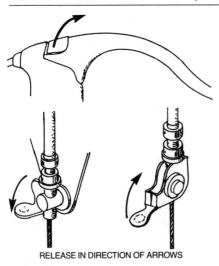

RELEASE IN DIRECTION OF ARROWS

2. To tighten up adjustment of the cable, back off on the locknut, screw the barrel adjuster out further, then hold the barrel adjuster in place with one hand, while tightening the locknut with the other.

3. If the adjusting range is inadequate, screw the adjuster in fully (back off the locknut all the way first), then undo the nut on the attachment bolt for the inner cable, pull the cable tauter using pliers, then tighten the nut on the attachment bolt again. Carry out a final adjustment with the barrel adjuster.

Note: Most brakes have a quick-release built in somewhere, with which the tension on the cable can be released. Use this to make adjusting easier, then tighten again after adjustment, and check whether the wheel is still free to turn and the adjustment indeed correct.

Note: Most mountain bikes and a few other models have an adjusting device built into the brake handle. Use it for regular adjustments.

Brake Shoe Adjustment and Replacement

Brake blocks can be used until they are almost completely worn off. I'd say, there is no need to replace the block as long as at least 3 mm (⅛ in) protrudes from the metal of the brake shoe holder. As the brake block material wears down, the position where it touches the rim will slowly change, and for this reason the attachment must be checked and corrected occasionally.

There are two basic types of brake shoes: those that can be adjusted up-and-down only, and those that can also be adjusted under a different angle, as shown in the illustration. In addition, some cantilever brakes have a spherical adjusting washer on the pivot, with which an angular adjustment of the front versus the rear portion is possible. Find out what type of adjustment you have, and adjust for optimal contact between the brake shoe and the side of the rim when the brake is pulled.

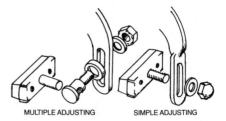

MULTIPLE ADJUSTING   SIMPLE ADJUSTING

When replacing the brake pad, it may not be possible to buy the block separately; in that case, you will have to replace the entire brake shoe with brake block installed. If you replace a brake shoe or install a new brake block in an old shoe with an open end, install it correctly as shown, so the brake block will not get pushed out of the shoe by the motion of the rim as you apply the brake. Make sure you get the right kind of brake shoe or block to fit your brake.

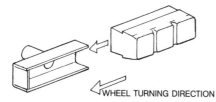

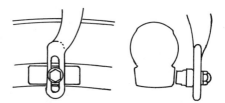

WHEEL TURNING DIRECTION

Lately, synthetic brake blocks have become popular, and these are certainly effective, although many cyclists prefer the more gradual braking provided by conventional rubber-based materials. Especially important when using synthetic brake blocks is keeping the sides of the rim meticulously clean, removing any trace of brake block material (especially after the brake was used extensively on a long descent) with solvent. The brake cable tension must always be adjusted anew after the brake shoe or the brake block is replaced (see preceding description).

Replace Brake Cable

The Bowden cable with which the hand brake is operated consists of an inner cable with a nipple that is held in the brake handle at one end, and a clamping bolt at the other end to hold it in the brake mechanism. It runs through a flexible spiral-wound outer cable. On some bikes the outer cable is a continuous length, on other bikes shorter pieces are used only where necessary, leaving straight sections of cable uncovered between stops brazed on to the bike. The ends of the sections of outer cable should be protected by ferrules, so the cable does not get pulled into the stop, which would render the brake ineffective – the plastic coating of the outer cable may have to be cut back far enough to accommodate the ferrule.

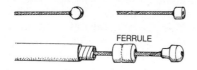

FERRULE

Tools and equipment
□ wrench to fit nut on brake cable clamp bolt
□ needle nose pliers
□ diagonal cutters or special cable cutters
□ lubricant (e.g. vaseline)
□ rag

Removal procedure

1. Release brake quick-release if installed; if not, release tension on the cable by screwing the adjuster in as far as possible.

2. Loosen the nut on the brake cable clamp bolt on the brake mechanism.

3. Pull the brake lever fully – this will release the inner and outer cables near the lever. Using the needle nose pliers, free the nipple from the internal recess in the brake lever, while the lever is pulled. Now remove inner and outer cable from the lever.

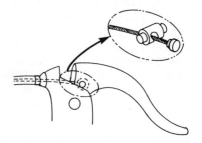

4. Pull the inner cable out in the direction of the nipple, catching any loose sections of outer cable and ferrules.

5. Inspect the outer cable to determine whether it can be reused. It should not be damaged or pinched anywhere, and should allow the inner cable to run through with minimal friction.

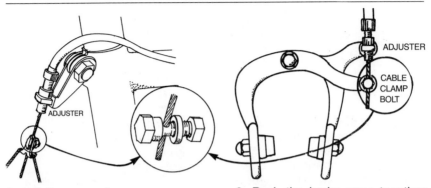

Installation procedure

1. Verify whether the new inner cable is long enough and whether it has the correct nipple for the brake handles used. Then lubricate the inner cable, using a vaseline-soaked rag.

2. Cut outer cable to length, making sure no hook is formed at the end; install ferrules.

3. Pull in the lever; insert the inner cable and hook the nipple on the recess inside the lever; then pull the cable taut, so the nipple stays in place when the lever is released. Keep the inner cable taut as you continue.

4. Push the inner cable through the outer cable. Install the latter so that no sharp bends are formed, even when turning the handlebars (at the front) and when pulling the brake (at the rear). Attach where appropriate.

5. Push the end of the inner cable through the cable clamp bolt; usually this is an eye bolt, i.e. a bolt with a hole through which the cable is inserted before the bolt is tightened to clamp it down.

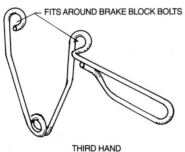

THIRD HAND

6. Push the brake arms together (either by hand, with a strap, or with a special tool, called third hand), pull the inner cable taut from behind the brake, while the clamp bolt is loose, then tighten the bolt. Cut off the inner cable about one inch beyond the clamp bolt (and solder together if you can).

7. Adjust the brake cable tension and brake operation as detailed in the preceding instruction *Rim Brake Adjustment,* making sure the adjustment is correct with the brake quick-release in the unreleased position.

Note: In the case of centerpull or cantilever brakes, also check the condition of the straddle cable (although some recently introduced brakes use solid linkages instead of the straddle cable).

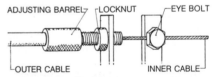

Replace or Overhaul Brake Lever

Brake levers should be matched both to the brake mechanism and to the handlebars used: even for the same brake, different levers are designed for drop handlebars and for straight or upright bars. Children's bikes should be equipped with levers designed for that specific purpose, since the child's hand is not generally big enough to reach an adult lever. Before removing or installing a brake lever, the handle-

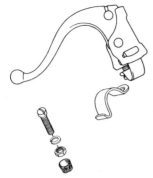

bar tape or the handgrips must be removed from the handlebars. It will be necessary to loosen the brake cable (as described above) if the lever is to be replaced by an other one. Refer to the exploded views for overhauling. Usually a stiff operating lever can be freed by replacing the bushings or by bending the metal around the pivot out a little. If not, you may have to replace the entire lever.

Tools and equipment
□ screwdriver (on some models Allen key) to fit the internal attachment bolt, reached when the lever is pulled

Removal procedure
1. Release tension on the brake cable (either with the quick-release, with the adjustment mechanism, or the cable attachment bolt).
2. Pull the lever; push the cable inside the lever to the side to gain access to the internal bolt. Loosen the bolt about three full turns – just not so far that it comes out of its special nut, since it would be hard to get back in before installing the lever. The strap with which the lever is clamped around the handlebars opens up a little this way.
3. Push the lever assembly off the handlebar ends, in a twisting movement if it becomes tight, loosening the bolt further if it will not come off any other way.

Installation procedure
1. Make sure the lever used is correct for the handlebars and the brake installed on the bike. Replace the cable if it is not in perfect condition.
2. Unscrew the internal bolt in the lever just far enough to loosen the attachment strap – not so far that it will come out of the special nut: if it does, it will be tricky to put it back in.
3. Slide the lever over the end of the handlebars into the right position. Check the position to make sure it can be reached and fully contracted easily with the whole hand – moving it further up or down the bend in the handlebars or angling it in or out will often improve these things. If the strap will not fit around the bars, it is the wrong size.
4. Tighten the bolt when the bars are in the right position; then install the cable as described above, making any adjustments to the brake that may be called for.
Note: Some cheap brake levers are attached with an external clamp. These are potential hazards, and I recommend replacing them by a model with a strap attachment as described here. If you must install the type with external clamp, it will be obvious how that's done.

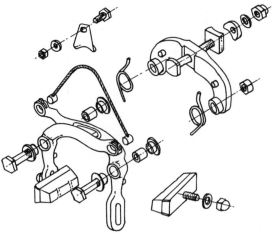

Replace or Overhaul Brake

If the brake itself does not give good performance, especially if it does not operate gradually or will not open up fully after having been applied, it should be overhauled or replaced. Before you do, check whether the problem may be alleviated by adjusting, cleaning, lubricating or replacing the control cable and the lever, since these are the more frequent causes of braking problems.

Tools and equipment
☐ wrench to fit attachment bolt
☐ wrench to fit nut on cable clamp bolt
☐ needle nose pliers
☐ to overhaul: small screwdriver and any wrenches to fit pivot bolts; lubricant

Removal procedure

1. Release tension on the brake cable (using quick-release, adjusting mechanism or cable clamp bolt). On centerpull and cantilever brakes, unhook the anchor plate from the straddle cable, and remove that cable.

2. Holding the brake mechanism in one hand, undo the mounting nut on the opposite side of the fork crown (front brake) or seat stay bridge (rear brake).

3. Remove the various spacers either side of the fork crown or seat stay bridge, while pulling the brake out of the hole. It may be necessary to release the cable altogether.

Overhauling procedure

I can give no step-by-step instructions for this work. Let the exploded views of the three most common brake types be your guide. Unhook and re-install the return springs, using the small screwdriver. Replace any bent or damaged parts (your bike shop may keep a bin of discarded parts from which you can often get the appropriate replacement). Replace the nylon or PTFE bushings at the pivots if they should be damaged. Clean and lubricate the various parts before re-assembling. Check for smooth operation and return movement before re-installing.

insert the bolt through the hole in the fork or the seat stay bridge; install the remaining spacers and washers; finally, install the nut.

3. Attach the cable, then adjust both cable and brake block position as described in the appropriate instructions above. Make sure the brake is installed straight, so both brake shoes are withdrawn equally far from the rim when the brake is released: loosen the mounting bolt slightly, straighten out, pull the lever firmly, hold the brake in that position, and tighten the bolt. Make final adjustments if necessary, and don't forget to put the quick-release in the tightened position.

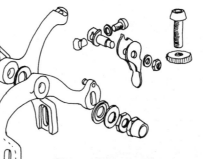

Installation procedure

1. Figure out where the various shaped spacers and washers should go. If you are installing a new brake, make sure the reach of the brake corresponds to the distance between the brake mounting hole and the position of the rim when the wheel is installed, and the brake is dimensioned to open up far enough to clear the width of the tire.

2. Put the washers or spacers that belong directly against the back of the brake in place on the mounting bolt;

Sidepull Brake Maintenance

Since on a sidepull brake the pivot bolt and the mounting bolt are the same, adjusting the one sometimes interferes with the other function. Two problems are quite common: excessive tightness (especially noticed when the brake arms do not return fully to the disengaged position) and unequal operation of the two brake arms. In the latter case, one brake shoe clears the rim much farther than the other; in fact, one may not clear it at all, especially if the rim is not perfectly straight.

To loosen up the pivot bolt, so the brake arms return fully when the lever is released, undo the outer locknut on the brake slightly; then, holding the brake firmly, loosen the underlying nut slightly (about 1/8 to 1/4 turn); finally, holding the brake and the inner bolt fixed, tighten the outer locknut. Check and readjust if necessary.

The operation of the brake arms can be evened out by centering the return spring. On some models this is achieved with a special centering wrench, with which either the mounting bolt assembly or just the boss in which the spring is held can be turned. The Take-a-Brake tool fits from the back of the brake in the spring coils, which can then be twisted. Tapping one side of the spring down with screwdriver and hammer while the brake lever is pulled sometimes works. If none of these methods solves the problem, proceed as follows to twist the mounting bolt complete with the spring:

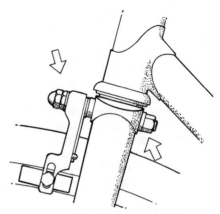

Tools and equipment

☐ wrench to fit locknut
☐ wrench to fit the underlying nut
☐ wrench to fit the attachment nut on the other side of the fork or seat stay bridge

Note: The mounting nut and the nut that lies under the locknut must be turned simultaneously, as must the locknut and the underlying nut, so you will indeed need several wrenches, even if the same size nut is used for two or more locations.

WEINMANN CENTERING TOOL

Procedure

1. Tighten the locknut and the underlying nut against one-another firmly; check to make sure the pivoting action is not diminished, and correct in accordance with the preceding description if necessary.

2. Holding the mounting nut with one wrench, and one of the other nuts (the locknut when turning clockwise, the nut that lies under the locknut when turning counterclockwise) with the

other, turn both simultaneously in the same direction towards which the brake arm action should be equalized.

3. Check and make any further adjustments that may be required.

Brake Squeal and Jitter

These two disturbing phenomena of rim brake operation are at opposite ends of the danger scale: squeal is quite harmless, and really little more than an embarrassment; brake jitter can disturb steering and balancing enough to cause a grave danger to the rider.

A squealing brake may be silenced by cleaning the rim, by choosing a different brake pad material, by using aluminum rims, rather than steel versions, or by toeing in the brake shoes somewhat. The latter operation brings the front end of the brake shoes a little closer to the rim than the back – the braking force will then straighten out the shoe again once the brake is applied. If the brake is not adjustable in this direction (some cantilever brakes

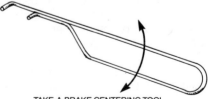

TAKE-A-BRAKE CENTERING TOOL

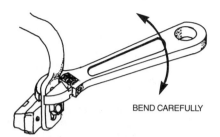

BEND CAREFULLY

have spherical inserts to do just that), you will have to bend the brake arm into the desired shape using two crescent wrenches – if you have the nerve for it.

Brake jitter is either caused by looseness in the brake mounting bolt or the pivots, by unevennesses in the side of the rim, or by excessive flexibility in the fork, and may be aggravated by loose head-set bearings. So those are the things to check and to correct, although at least one of these factors – flexibility in the fork – can not be eliminated, except by replacing the entire fork. In my experience, fork flexibility should only be seen as an aggravating factor, increasing the effect of other ones: when the other problem is corrected, the brake will not jitter, even with the flexible fork. It is likely that choosing different brake block materials may also alleviate the problem to some extent – experiment around, once you have eliminated the most dangerous causes and the symptoms have not completely disappeared.

Extension Levers

Many cheaper ten-speed bikes come equipped with extension levers, with which the brakes can be operated from the top of the drop handlebar. The soundest advice is probably to remove them, yet many riders feel safer with them, and my zeal for their reform is less firm than my desire to at least teach them how these things should be used to best advantage.

There are different types, but almost all work similarly, pivoted around the main brake lever pivot point, and the other lever either inserted between the brake lever mount and the lever proper, or attached directly to another pivot on the lever. Adjust the brake lever assembly in such a way that both the regular lever and the extension lever can be reached comfortably and will not bottom out before the brake is applied fully as described in the checking procedure under *Rim Brake Adjustments*. This usually requires moving the lever attachment to a slightly different position and angle on the bend of the handlebars, and that may require shifting or replacing the handlebar tape. Extension levers are not usually very rigid (which is also their inherent drawback), so it will be possible to bend them into a more favorable shape. When you are in an emergency, and have to brake very hard and suddenly, you should use the regular brake lever, so that full braking force is applied. If you remove the extension, also replace the overlong pivot bolt by a regular model to avoid injury.

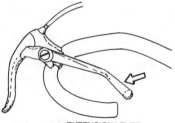

EXTENSION LEVER

Brake Hoods

Brake levers for drop handlebars without extension levers generally come equipped with soft rubber hoods. These provide significant comfort when riding in such a position that the hands are just on top of the brake lever mounts. Install, replace or remove the hood when the cable is disconnected. When you remove the extension levers, I suggest you add such a rubber hood at the time – almost any make of hood will fit any make of lever, providing a regular brake lever pivot bolt is installed. When installing handlebar tape, lift up the hood to allow you to wrap closely around the brake lever mount.

Tandem Brakes

Most tandems are (and indeed should be) equipped with three brakes. As a rule, two rim brakes – usually of the cantilever design – are used in combination with a drum brake on the rear wheel hub. All these brakes are operated from the front handlebars, leaving you more handles than hands, if normal levers are chosen. There are levers on the market which allow attaching two cables side-by-side. It is usually recommended to control the front rim brake separately with one lever, the two rear brakes together with the other.

Conversely, you may consider the rear hub brake separately altogether, controlling it from a separate lever, such as a so-called guidonnet lever mounted in the middle of the handlebars or a 'panic lever' operated by the rider in the rear (referred to as stoker, while the one in the front is called captain in bicycle jargon). It is even possible to operate the rear drum

brake from a handlebar-end mounted gear shift lever, as long as its pivot bolt is adjusted so tightly that it will indeed hold adequately to retard the bike on a long descent. Of course, you'll still use the rim brakes in an emergency.

Drum Brakes

The drum brake is an internal expanding brake, operating inside a widened part of the hub. Although they are quite commonly installed on regular utility bikes in some countries, they are almost exclusively seen on the rear wheels of tandems in the US and Britain. Their advantage is that they are not sensitive to rain, and – as opposed to the coaster brake – work on both the front and the rear wheel.

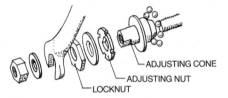

— ADJUSTING CONE
— ADJUSTING NUT
└ LOCKNUT

DRUM BRAKE BEARING ADJUSTING DETAILS

As far as maintenance on these brakes is concerned, they should be adjusted similarly to rim brakes. Cable and control lever work is also similar. Once or twice a year, take the thing apart (starting at the side of the operating lever) and check the condition of the brake shoes: they must be at least 3 mm (⅛ in) thick at their thinnest

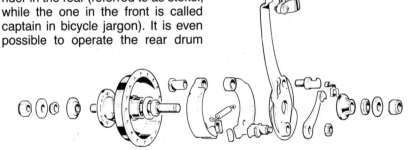

point; if they are held with rivets, these must lie at least 1.5 mm (¹⁄₁₆ in) below the surface. When they are worn, they may be relined at any brake maintenance shop. Keep lubricants and solvents off the brake shoes; when reinstalling, put just a little grease on the pivot and the cam-shaped device which opens the brake segments up. Check the springs that return the segments to the inactive position, and lubricate and adjust the ball bearings at that time. Attach the lever to the fork or the stay when installing the brake, then adjust the cable tension.

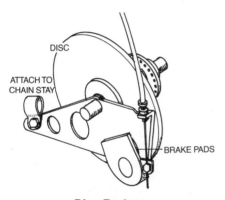

Disc Brakes

Disc brakes are even rarer than drum brakes, although they too are found on some tandems, and then also mainly on the rear wheel. I suggest requesting maintenance instructions from the manufacturer, if these were not supplied with the bike in the first place, since they vary quite a bit as regards construction details. Most important is to check the cable tension adjustment as for regular rim brakes, and to make sure the disc does not get bent or otherwise damaged. Occasionally, clean the disc itself with a clean rag soaked in solvent, taking great care not to get any solvent or grease on the brake pads. As with all other hub brakes, the lever that connects the fixed part of the brake to the frame

must be kept well tightened and securely reinstalled after any wheel removal or adjustment.

The Coaster Brake

Several different designs of coaster brake are in use, and for that reason it is not possible to provide detailed instructions for the maintenance of the hub itself. Most often, the work required amounts to no more than adjustment or lubrication of the bearings. To adjust the bearings of a coaster brake, so the wheel turns freely without noticeable lateral play, loosen the axle nut on the left side. Using a fitting wrench (a special wrench is supplied with most models), tighten the cone, then the locknut, and finally fasten the axle nut again. On some models the axle has a square end on the RH side – turning the axle with the special wrench at this square end will have the same effect as turning the cone and the locknut. To overhaul and lubricate the bearings, remove the wheel from the bike, then undo the locknuts and cones on both sides, proceeding as for any other wheel bearing overhauling work.

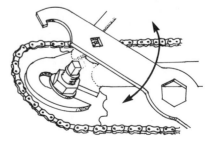

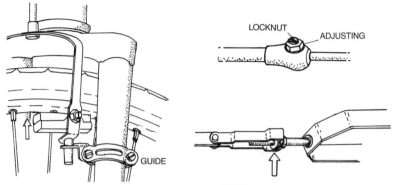

STIRRUP (ROLLER-LEVER) BRAKE

Stirrup Brakes

Stirrup brakes, also called roller-lever brakes, are operated by means of a system of pivoting levers, attached to the frame. Check the attachments and lubricate the pivots from time to time. Straighten out any section of control rod that may have been bent. When the handlebars are removed or readjusted, the rod connectors must be loosened and subsequently reinstalled. Similarly, the brake shoes have to be removed and reinstalled whenever the wheel is removed from the bike. After any such work – and whenever the brake requires adjustment for other reasons – readjust by means of the round, knurled adjusting nuts shown in the illustrations. If the adjusting range of these is exceeded, screw them all the way out; then undo the rod connector, reconnecting it to shorten the rod, and finally use the knurled nut for fine-tuning. Most other care and maintenance recommendations are the same as those given for regular rim brakes elsewhere in this chapter.

Special Rim Brakes

In recent years several special rim brakes have been introduced, primarily for mountain bike use. These include SunTour's cam-operated models with fixed pivots, and centerpull variants with fixed pivot bosses by Shimano and Dia Compe. The former are suitable for use on front and rear wheels, the latter only for the rear. For rear wheel use, all are generally installed below the chain stays.

Their maintenance is nothing very much out of the ordinary. Be guided by the preceding remarks pertaining to centerpull and cantilever brakes. On the cam-operated models, the brake is released (e.g. to remove the wheel) by pushing the brake shoes together and twisting the cam plate out from between the rollers. Cleaning, lubrication and adjustment are generally enough to keep these things working.

An entirely different kettle of fish is Scott-Matthauser's new hydraulic brake. This seems to be the ultimate brake on the market, but is as yet too new to have accumulated maintenance experience. Refer any problems you may encounter to the manufacturer via your bike shop.

11
Accessories

Although it will not be possible to give very detailed maintenance instructions for every conceivable accessory that can be attached to a bicycle, I shall at least try to cover the most important ones here: lighting, luggage racks (in Britain: carriers), fenders (mudguards), kick stand (prop stand) and pump. Many other items come with the manufacturer's maintenance instructions, which should be followed for best results.

Generator Lights

This is in my opinion the most convenient and reliable form of lighting. It consists of a wheel-driven generator (dynamo in Britain), which supplies electricity to a separate head light and a rear light via insulated cables. The electricity is carried back to the generator via the earthing or mass connectors on lights and generator through the metal of the bicycle frame. By way of regular maintenance, try out the system from time to time (ideally every day, since it is really not much trouble): engage the generator, lift up and turn the wheel on which the generator operates fast, and while the wheel is turning, look (or let someone else do it for you) to verify whether both lights burn brightly. If something is amiss, proceed to the fault-finding diagram below.

Adjust the alignment of the generator as shown in the accompanying illustrations. The centerline through the generator should coincide with an imaginary line from te wheel axle to the generator roller. The roller should engage a rubberized part of the tire (if necessary, correct by moving the mounting hardware or bending it to suit), and should contact the tire over its entire width. A rubber cap may be installed on the roller to improve contact with the tire in wet weather and to limit damage to the tire. Disengaged, the distance between the roller and the tire should be about 5–8 mm ($\frac{3}{16}$ to $\frac{5}{16}$ in). All nuts and bolts must be tightened and the mechanism lubricated. Check to make sure the electric cables are intact and fastened to the contacts at generator and lamp units.

Most trouble-prone on generator lighting systems are the pinch screws which provide the mass or earthing contact for most types. Rust and dirt play havoc with electric contacts of this kind, and I consequently favor replacing them with a second set of cables. Use either complete double wiring or partial double wiring. In the first case, double wires run from the generator to each of the lamp units; in the latter case, merely make an additional wire connection between

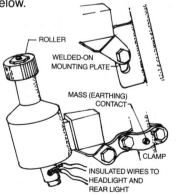

ROLLER
WELDED-ON MOUNTING PLATE
MASS (EARTHING) CONTACT
CLAMP
INSULATED WIRES TO HEADLIGHT AND REAR LIGHT

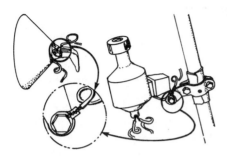

the mass of the generator and a bolt that has good contact with the metal of the bike frame. See the instructions in Chapter 2 for soldering the wire ends to obtain more reliable contacts.

Troubleshooting

A systematic method of fault-finding is contained in the accompanying diagram. This is a primitive form of logic diagram, and I hope readers familiar with such devices will not object to the substitution of familiar symbols by mere rectangles, which is predicated on space limitations (and to some extent on the desire not to scare off the less initiated).

Bulb Replacement

Most generator lighting systems rely on miniature bulbs with screwed lamp bases, although in Britain bayonet bases are also in use. If in doubt, check what type of bulbs are used. For a conventional 6 volt, 3 watt system, use a 6 volt, 2.4 watt (also known as 6 volt, 0.4 amp) bulb in the front and a 6 volt, 0.6 watt (or 6 volt, 0.1 amp) bulb in the rear. These bulbs are designed to give optimal performance consistant with a reasonable lamp life at relatively low cycling speeds. If you habitually ride faster, you may find you burn out a lot of bulbs. In that case you may be able to find bulbs that draw slightly more current (i.e.

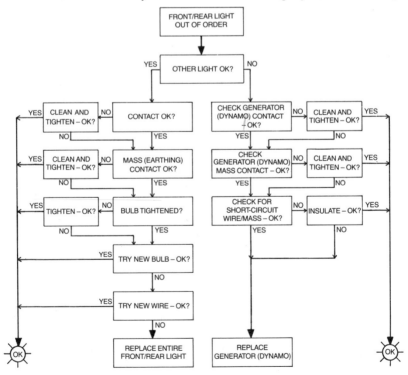

have a somewhat higher wattage or amperage rating at the same voltage) to be of some benefit.

In recent years halogen cycle bulbs and krypton-filled bulbs have been introduced by a number of manufacturers. These provide a more consistant light output over the life of the bulb, since they do not suffer the blackening effect on the inside of the glass bulb which dulls conventional bulbs. In addition, the halogen-cycle bulb actually has a higher light output from the start. Halogen bulbs should only be installed in units designed for their use, whereas krypton-filled bulbs can be used as (expensive) replacements for conventional bulbs. Halogen bulbs are very sensitive to excess voltage, so should only be used if a voltage control device is built in with the lamp housing or the generator.

Hub generator
Though the best known example of the wheel hub with built-in generator, the Sturmey-Archer Dyno-Hub, is no longer made, enough of these units are still around to justify maintenance instructions. Since their output is lower than that of regular generators, they should be used with the special bulbs supplied for this purpose. The Dyno-Hub requires double wiring, a

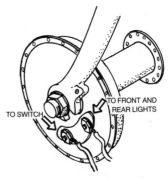

HUB GENERATOR (DYNAMO)

special switch, and an installation that insulates the wiring entirely from the mass of the bicycle frame. See the illustration for wiring instructions. To prevent frequent burning out of bulbs, make sure you don't ride with the light switched on by daylight (which you will not notice as easily with this mechanically efficient device as with a conventional generator).

Bottom Bracket Mounted Roller Generator
This type of generator is also mechanically more efficient than the conventional tire-driven generator (so, again, take care to switch it off when not needed). It is mounted under the chain stays, just behind the bottom bracket, rolling against the tread of the tire. This is a location that attracts a lot of dirt and water, leading to frequent malfunctioning of the mechanism. Keep it clean and lubricated to minimize these problems. Depending on the dimensions of the bicycle frame, you may have to use a file to remove enough of the soft aluminum of the generator mount to install it properly. You may also have to push the rear wheel relatively far forward in the drop-outs to provide adequate contact between the tire and the roller.

Two additional tricks are sometimes necessary to get satisfactory performance from this kind of equipment in

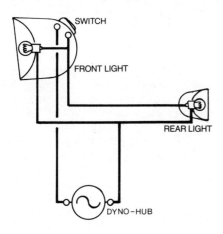

SWITCH

FRONT LIGHT

REAR LIGHT

DYNO-HUB

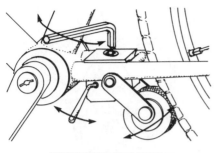

ROLLER GENERATOR (DYNAMO)

wet weather. The simplest one is to attach a spring or a loop of elastic band between the arms that hold the roller and the rear drop-out to increase the force with which the roller is pushed against the tire. The second method is to install a material with a higher coefficient of friction over the roller. You may use a section of an old inner tube (which can be installed when you disassemble the arms that hold the roller), or you can use self-adhesive non-skid material, as sold for use in a bath tub. Seal the seam with e.g. silicone bathtub caulk.

Battery Lights
Although battery lighting is simpler than generator lighting, not relying on so many wires and contacts, it is often plagued by similar problems. If it doesn't work, first check the bulb with the unit's own batteries (using a piece of metal wire to provide a direct contact). If it doesn't work, check whether the bulb or the battery is at fault, by checking the same bulb with the battery of the other lighting unit. Always carry along fully charged spare batteries and a spare bulb for replacement purposes.

If neither bulb nor battery are at fault, it must be a matter of internal contacts within the lamp housing. Clean all metal contacts with sandpaper and protect them with special battery terminal grease or simply with acid-free vaseline. You may also have

to bend a lamp housing contact in or out to reach the bulb, battery or switch contact. If all else fails, you may have to make a provisional contact with a piece of electrical wire or a metal strip.

Light Adjustment
Install or adjust the mounting of a headlight in such a way that it satisfies these criteria:
☐ It must illuminate the road ahead of the bike.
☐ It must be visible to other road users.
☐ It may not blind other road users.
The best way to achieve that is by mounting the light relatively high and aiming it down to a point about 30 feet ahead of the bike. Tighten the various mounting bolts adequately to avoid accidental misalignment, yet not so tight as to preclude intentional readjustment.

The rear light should also be mounted so as to be highly visible to others. Again, a high mounting position is most favorable. Since it is not quite so bright as a head light, it must not be aimed down, but should point straight back. Make sure it does not get obstructed by luggage mounted on the back of the bike. Tighten the mounting bolts fully – there'll be no need to readjust the rear light.

Reflectors
Even reflectors require some maintenance. The only really important reflector on a bicycle is the one in the back, facing back, since that is the only one that serves a purpose not better served by other equipment. If you have a front light, you don't need a front reflector – and if you don't have a front light, you shouldn't be riding out at night. Spoke reflectors are not visible to the only vehicles that might endanger you from the side – namely those that are in a side street or driveway ahead of you, *before* their headlights shine on your bike. Pedal reflec-

tors are merely an inferior substitute for a big rear reflector. So you may remove any one of the other reflectors, as long as you install, adjust, check and, if necessary, replace the one in the back.

A reflector loses its capacity to reflect light back to its source (the only thing it can do in the first place – so that's why reflectors are only useful to those whose own headlights are aimed at your bike) if moisture penetrates between the translucent plastic and the inside of the case. Moisture is likely to penetrate whenever there's a crack in either the base or the reflective element. So you must replace a cracked reflector immediately.

To check whether a reflector is doing its job, place the bike 30 ft ahead of a car with its headlights on. If the reflector lights up brightly as seen from the driver's seat, it is fine. If it doesn't, it should be replaced. Attach reflectors firmly and perpendicular to the horizontal. Some reflectors (specifically those that comply with the CPSC regulations for toy bicycles, which, by the way, are not better but poorer than standard modern highway marker reflectors to SAE standards), have an arrow showing which end should be mounted at the top. Comply with this marking, since these models may not otherwise be visible to drivers following closely.

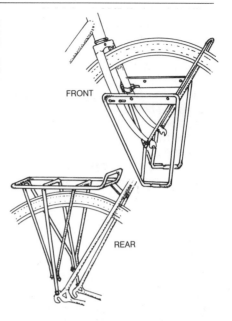

FRONT

REAR

Luggage Racks

Luggage racks, or carriers, as they are called in Britain, are available for the rear and (less commonly) for the front of the bike. Keep the rack properly fastened to the bike and replace it when it is broken. At the drop-outs, the stays for the rack should be mounted directly against the drop-outs: do not mount other items (e.g. the stays of fenders) between the two.

If the rack does not attach to brazed-on eyelets on the bike, mounting clamps are used. Before installing such a clamp, wrap the bike tubing with a rubber patch from the tire patch kit, cemented in the right position with rubber solution. This will protect the bike and provide a firm attachment that will not slip or come loose as easily as might otherwise be the case. This is especially important in the front, where the tapered shape of the fork blades would not hold the clamp in place very well.

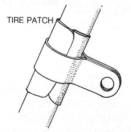

TIRE PATCH

The front rack is best attached to the back of the fork crown. I have heard horror stories of the brake bolt on which the rack is mounted coming loose on models attached to the front of the fork crown, which resulted in the entire rack coming off towards the front, jamming up the front wheel and hurting the rider. Though you should really notice things like this before they get out of hand (surely you should notice the front brake is acting up long before the bolt is completely loose), it does serve to illustrate that the mounting bolt must be checked and tightened, especially if the rack is mounted on the front of the fork crown. It may even be reasonable to tie the rack around the fork crown with a strap.

Fenders

These items don't seem to find much favor in American eyes. To increase your bicycle's usefulness, it will still be a good idea to mount fenders, since riding in the rain without is torture, yet it turns out to be quite tolerable with them. If you prefer a temporary installation, replace the single nut on the front and rear brake bolts by sets of two thin locknuts (always use these in pairs for adequate strength), mounting the rack's attachment clip between the two. Make your own wingnuts (or rather wing bolts) to facilitate removal and installation at the drop-outs, using a regular round-headed screw bolt and a sizable washer, soldered into the slot.

SOLDER WASHER IN SLOT

As for maintenance, keep the attachments tightened and the stays straight, so the fenders don't interfere with the wheels. Cut any protruding ends of the mounting stays short with diagonal cutters. The mounting hardware provided in the USA – in order to comply with one of the CPSC toy bicycle requirements – is designed to be mounted with the stays *inside* the fender or its bracket. This generally

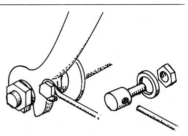

brings the stays too close to the tires. A little imagination will usually allow you to mount them differently, so that the stays are on the outside. When mounting fenders, keep them radially about a cm (⅜ in) away from the tire – not more, since the front one would then interfere with the tip of your foot when cornering at low speed.

Kick Stand

The most common kind of kick stand (called prop stand in Britain) is mounted between the chain stays, and hinges to one side of the bike. It is either mounted directly to a flat plate that takes the place of the tubing bridge between the stays (on some cheap bikes) or it is clamped around the stays. The clamped type will stay in place better if the stays are first covered with a big patch from the tire patch kit, installed with rubber solution just as you would mend a puncture. Keep the thing tightened and, if it is bent out, first loosen the attachment bolt before trying to straighten it out, then install it properly. An 8 mm Allen wrench (not used anywhere else on the bike, and a heavy chunk of metal to carry around) is used to work on

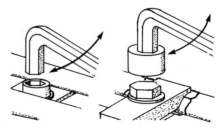

most kick stands, although some models have a regular bolt that can only be operated with a (very big) socket wrench.

Other Accessories

As promised, no detailed instructions for the care of other gadgets that may be hung on the bike. Let the message be brief: if it moves, lubricate it; if it shouldn't move, tighten it. What's lubricated should be wiped clean afterwards. What's tightened should always be held in at least two points, so it won't come loose again accidentally. Use a washer under every nut, and use a locknut or locking adhesive to hold down particularly vibration-prone nuts. For any more detailed maintenance instructions, refer to the manufacturer's information that accompanies most accessories.

Pump

It's the one tool you can't do without. Gas stations are not always at hand when you have a flat or otherwise need to inflate the tires. Besides, if you use tires with Presta valves, which are much easier to inflate, the hose connector at the gas station won't fit. Although adaptor nipples exist, they have their problems too, as explained below.

The connector or head of the pump should also correspond to the valve used on the bike. If it does not work properly, either the rubber washer at the connector is worn out, or the plunger inside the pump does not fully close off the pump tube. Take it apart and bend the plunger out, applying a little lubricant. The washer in the connector can be replaced – it too should be impregnated with grease if it is leather, glycerine if natural rubber, vaseline if plastic.

ADAPTOR

DRILL OUT TO CLEAR VALVE MECHANISM

Pumps with connector tubes are not very satisfactory, since the air in the tube limits the pressure to which the pump can operate, and since the additional connector at the tube tends to leak. Adaptors to use one type of pump on another type of tire valve often leak, too. It may help to drill out the hole inside the adaptor, so the internals of the Presta valve will fit inside with better clearance.

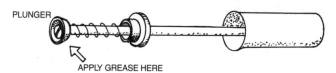

PLUNGER

APPLY GREASE HERE

12
Painting a Bicycle

In this chapter I shall give some advice to those readers who want to repaint an old bicycle or touch up paint that is scratched. The best advice to those who are tempted to repaint their entire frame is probably, *don't*. It is extremely time-consuming and demanding work, which at best produces acceptable results; at the worst it may be a total disaster. Heed the advice in this chapter to improve your chances of success, but don't expect your first attempt to look really satisfactory, though your skills will improve with time and practice.

Touch-up Painting

If my enthusiasm about completely repainting a bike is limited, I do encourage anyone to touch up the paint of his bicycle when it is scratched or chipped. This is simple work that, conscientiously executed, will keep your bike looking good a long time. What you need for the job is a small bottle of matching touch-up paint, a brush, sandpaper, a clean rag and paint thinner or terpentine. The best time to buy matching touch-up paint is when you buy the bike, since manufacturers often revise their color schemes and rarely are eager to supply touch-up paint for a bike that was sold a long time ago. This is a good reason to buy a bike from a major manufacturer (who is more likely to supply touch-up paint in the first place) or to choose any one of the colors in which Henry Ford offered his model T, namely black.

The paint thinner must be selected for compatibility with the kind of paint used. For most ordinary paints that means terpentine, but some modern paints should only be used with specific different solvents – read the instructions for the paint. As for the other necessities, the cloth must be lint-free and soft, the brush must have fine short bristles, and the sandpaper must be very fine. Do the work whenever you will not need the bike for a couple of days, so the paint has enough time to cure.

Procedure

1. Clean the bike (or at a minimum the area around the scratch to be treated) before starting the job. Then sandpaper the damaged area to bare metal, removing any rust. To do that, take a small piece of sandpaper, folded into an even smaller pad.

2. Wipe the sanded area clean with a dry cloth, then use a clean part of the rag, soaked in solvent, to clean it thoroughly. Wipe once more with a dry part of the rag. This will remove any dirt or grease that might impair adhesion of the paint.

3. Stir the paint thoroughly, mixing the thinner upper layers well with the thicker lower layer of the contents of the can. If the paint was supplied in a spray can, shake the can well, then spray a 'puddle' of paint, concentrated in one place in a small receptacle such as a bottle cap.

4. Dip the tip of the brush in the paint and apply only in the area where the paint was removed (don't overlap).

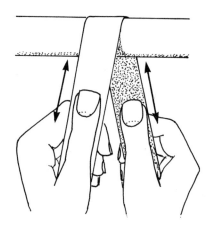

5. Clean the brush in solvent. Let the paint cure at least 24 hours before using the bike.

Note: It is preferable to use two applications of paint: the first one with a primer, which must be compatible with the kind of finish paint used; it must be allowed to cure 24 hours before you apply the finish coat. This will generally improve adhesion and durability.

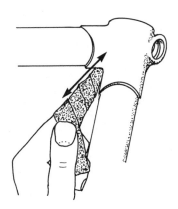

Repainting the Frame

Before starting this job, be sure you really want to: you'll have to put in a lot of work and you'll be without the bike for several weeks. Your bike shop can probably recommend a paintshop which will do a better job more quickly, at a price that is low considering the amount of work and time you will be investing yourself. If you insist, follow these procedures.

The job can be broken down into several stages: preparation, priming, painting, curing and finishing. Probably the most time consuming part in terms of man-hours is preparation; in terms of total elapsed time, curing takes the longest.

Preparation

Before you start, remove all parts until you have nothing but a bare frame left. Also remove the bearing cups of the head-set and the bottom bracket as described in Chapters 4 and 6.

Now the old paint and any rust that has formed must be removed. Do the work in a well ventilated area (a sheltered outside area is probably best). The easiest way is to use a chemical paint stripper, following the instructions on the can and taking care not to get the stuff on your skin and not to breathe in the fumes. Smear it on generously, let it penetrate until the paint is soft and wrinkled, then scrape it off with a putty knife and wash off any remnants, using plenty of water and a hard brush. Repeat for areas where the paint was not completely removed the first time. Wipe dry after rinsing.

Using fine wet-or-dry sandpaper, which you soak in water to remove the embedded particles frequently, remove the last spots of paint. After that, sand the entire frame with dry sandpaper of the same type until you are down to shiny blank metal everywhere. Use strips of sandpaper about 1–2 in wide for the tubes, narrower strips, wrapped around your finger as shown, to get into all the nooks and crannies. When completed, wipe with a solvent-soaked rag, then with a dry rag. The solvent must be compatible with the particular paint that will be used (check with the store where you buy the paint).

You can save yourself a lot of this work if you can find a shop that will sandblast the frame for you, preferably using fine glass beads, which are less damaging to the metal surface than angular grit or sand. Since especially expensive bicycles are made of thin tubing, excessive sandblasting should be avoided, as it might remove too much metal in critical spots. Wash the sandblasted frame with solvent and then wipe it dry.

Priming

Select a primer that is of a similar color as the finish coat paint and of a compatible type (i.e. based on the same solvent). If the same color is not available, use a light grey for light shades of paint, a dark grey for dark shades. I usually make two applications of primer, and I thin the paint by adding about 10–20% additional solvent. This will result in a thinner and more even layer of primer.

Between applications, and after the final application, allow the paint to cure at least 24 hours, then sand down to a smooth surface with wet-or-dry sandpaper, washing it out frequently to remove the paint particles that become embedded in the sandpaper. The primer itself can be applied with a brush; use a flat brush, about 1 in wide for the larger tubes, a narrower brush for the tight spots. If you can get primer in a spray can, you may choose to use that, providing you practice first, because it is quite tricky to spray an even layer and to cover everywhere. For more advice on spraying, refer to the section *Finish Coat Painting*, below.

Do this and all painting work in a clean, well ventilated area at temperatures above 10°C (50°F). A sheltered outside area, such as a back porch, is very suitable, providing there is no wind to blow up dust that would ruin the smoothness of the paint.

After completion of the priming and sanding, wash the frame off with a rag, soaked in clean solvent, then dry with a lint-free rag.

Finish Coat Painting

Although it is possible to use a brush for this work, it will be easier and the result will look better if you use a spray can. Even better would be to use proper spray painting equipment, preferably of the airless variety, which splutters less and gives a smoother coating.

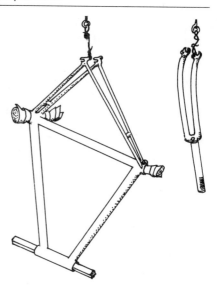

Although you can use any spray paint, I have found the ones sold by Schwinn for use on their bicycles particularly suitable, since they seem to cure harder and faster than most regular spray can paints.

Before you ruin the bike, learn to handle the spray can, trying it out on some other tubular metal construction. Start spraying outside the object to be painted, then move the hand with the spray can evenly over the entire length, finishing beyond the item to be painted. If you were to start spraying while the can is aimed at the bike, or to reverse motion while the can is still aimed at the bike, the paint would be too thick in those places. Work all around each tube, overlapping each next application until each tube is evenly coated all around, before moving on to the next tube. First do the main tubes, then go on to the rear triangles.

If you do it right, there will be no unpainted areas left in the corners, the lugs and the drop-outs. It will be particularly tricky to touch up such areas later if you don't cover them at the same time as you paint the main tubes, so try to get them covered right away. If you do have to touch up such spots, do it the same way, starting outside the bike, covering the unpainted spot while moving the can along and reversing outside the bike.

While doing the painting, you must not touch the bike. Hang up the frame and the fork as shown in the illustration; use the stick to turn the frame in the appropriate orientation. Put old newspaper or a drop cloth under and behind the job, so you don't get paint everywhere. It will be a good idea to wear a mask to avoid breathing in the fumes and paint particles.

There are two entirely different ways of painting, using enamel and lacquer, respectively. Enamel consists of a lot of pigment with a little solvent, which goes on in one or two relatively thick layers. Lacquer is a lot of solvent with relatively little pigment, and requires many more layers, which can be applied within relatively short intervals.

Curing

Certainly when using enamel, the paint must be allowed to cure very well before the last coat is applied, as it must afterwards, before it is hard enough to handle the bike.

Don't do anything to the bike until the paint is hard, allowing it to cure at least as long as is recommended in the instructions for the paint. Curing must be done in a clean, dry and preferably warm room. When you think the paint is really quite hard, . . . wait a few more days before touching it, because even when the surface feels dry, the paint underneath will still be quite soft and easily ruined.

Finishing

When the paint is finally cured, you may very carefully polish the paint with paint polish, which is a very mild abrasive in liquid solution. Rubbing compound is slightly more abbrasive and may only be used on older paint that has been cured several months. After polishing, wash the bike with clean water, wipe it dry and then apply a coat of transparent lacquer. This will provide a harder surface layer and will keep the paint looking bright and shiny longer. Allow the transparent lacquer to harden at least 24 hours before you start reassembling the bike, still taking great care not to scratch the paint when doing so.

If you want certain areas of the bike to be painted in a different color, first paint the smaller sections in the secondary color, overlapping onto the neighboring areas if necessary to cover the proper parts completely. Allow this paint to cure, then cover the part that will remain that color with paper and tape, and paint the rest of the bike, overlapping the taped-off area where necessary.

To apply pin stripes, e.g. highlighting the contours of the lugs, first paint the entire frame and allow to dry completely. Then use a very fine brush with short bristles to apply the contrasting lines.

To apply transfers, wait until the paint is cured, polish and wash the area where the transfer will go, then put on the transfers, following the manufacturer's instruction. If you finish the bike with transparent lacquer, do that *after* the transfers are in place.

13
Home-Made Tools and Equipment

In addition to, or in place of, the tools mentioned elsewhere in the book, I suggest making several items yourself. Most of these are aids that will make working on the bike easier; others are things that will protect your bike. No detailed instructions, merely proposal sketches with brief descriptions.

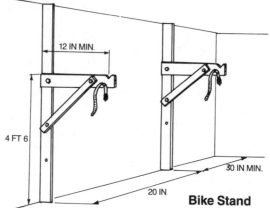

12 IN MIN.

4 FT 6

30 IN MIN.

20 IN

Bike Stand

Raises the bike off the ground while you are working on it. May be mounted free-standing or against the wall. Wooden boards, wood scraps, wood screws will be required.

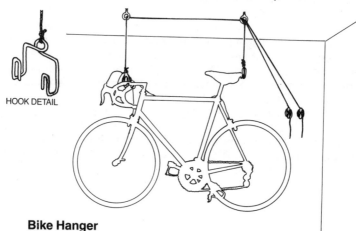

HOOK DETAIL

Bike Hanger

Another device for the same job. Rope, screw eyes and hooks bent out of steel wire will be required.

Handlebar Support

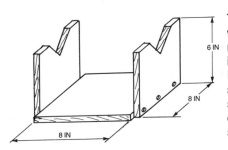

To support the bike by the handlebars when it is turned upside-down, so it is raised high enough not to damage items mounted on the handlebars. Particularly useful for work on ten-speed bikes with drop handlebars, since it prevents damage to the brake cables. Wood scraps and wood screws are all you need.

Wheel Centering Gauge

This tool allows you to compare the distance between the rim and the locknuts on both sides of the wheel. A ruler, wooden board, wood screws and wood scraps are needed.

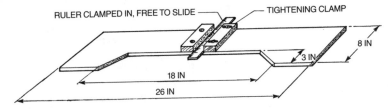

RULER CLAMPED IN, FREE TO SLIDE — TIGHTENING CLAMP

8 IN

3 IN

18 IN

26 IN

Lighting Test Board

A handy item to trace faults in the electric components of any lighting system. Use a 4.5 V or 6 V battery, a switch, 6 V bulb with fitting, connector strips, alligator clips (in Britain: crocodile clips), electric wires and a small board with woodscrews and some scrap metal.

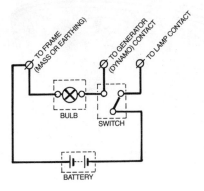

TO FRAME (MASS OR EARTHING)
TO GENERATOR (DYNAMO) CONTACT
TO LAMP CONTACT
BULB
SWITCH
BATTERY

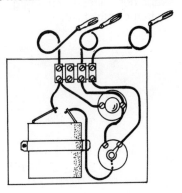

Saddle Cover

Neater and more durable than a plastic bag, this item will keep your saddle dry when you park your bike in the rain. Waterproof coated fabric, elastic band and webbing straps are all that's needed.

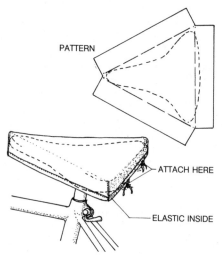

PATTERN

ATTACH HERE

ELASTIC INSIDE

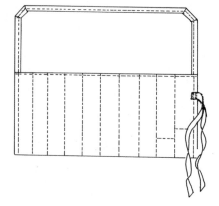

Tool Pouch

A handy organizer for your tools. Before you make it, select exactly those tools you will want to take along, then lay them out with enough space between them to allow you to roll the whole thing up. Any sturdy fabric (I use an old pair of jeans) and a piece of webbing strap is all you'll need.

Bicycle Carrying Bag

Hidden in this bag, your bike can go many places where it would not otherwise be admitted. Use light coated nylon fabric, Velcro tape and webbing straps. Note that the carrying straps don't attach to the bag, but to the frame of the bike.

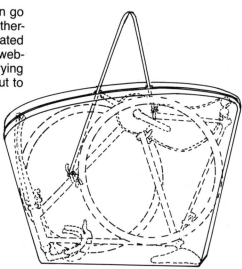

Appendix

Further Reading

You will hardly believe how many books have been written about the bicycle and its maintenance. This book was written with the intention of providing the most comprehensive, compact guide to essential repairs. Yet you may encounter certain problems which are not covered as thoroughly here as you may like. For such instances, and for those readers who are more curious about other aspects of the bicycle, here is a summary of the most useful books on the market today.

R. Ballantine, *Richard's Bicycle Book*. Ballantine Books, New York; Pan Books, London.

One of the first good popular bicycle books, with excellent illustrations and clear (though not always scientifically correct) instructions for repairs and maintenance, only marred by the author's ignorance of some of the technical and non-technical matters about which he nevertheless feels obliged to propound a strong opinion.

J. Brandt, *The Bicycle Wheel*. Avocet, Palo Alto (CA).

An entire book devoted to nothing but the bicycle wheel – how to select, maintain and repair it. Fascinating for the technically curious and very thorough in its treatment of wheelbuilding.

C.W. Coles and H.T. Glenn, *Glenn's Complete Bicycle Manual*. Crown Publishers, New York.

Recently updated by John Allen, this is the most complete bicycle repair handbook, illustrated with photographs and very systematically arranged. Not always clear, and often confusing, yet an excellent back-up source for any kind of overhauling work, including some of the more gutsy items, like gear hubs and special brakes.

T. Cuthberson, *Anybody's Bike Book*. Ten-Speed Press, Berkely (CA).

A laid-back guide to the bicycle and most of the essential repair and maintainance jobs. Well written and simple to follow, this is the book to use if you're not very ambitious in bicycle technical matters, yet want to do your own maintenance work.

F. DeLong, *DeLong's Guide to Bicycles and Bicycling*. Chilton Books, Radnor (PA).

The most thorough technical bicycle book ever written in English (ignoring the purely theoretical works). It is not very useful as a repair guide, but gives a lot of insight into the causes of technical problems. This helps the reader understand the bicycle and its problems well enough to make step-by-step repair instructions superfluous – providing he cares to read through this much material.

E. A. Sloane, *The New Complete Book of Bicycling*. Simon and Schuster, New York.

The biggest and the fattest bike book ever. Full of useful and trivial details, ranging from touring to racing and from repairing to selection of camping gear. It is probably the best written book of its kind, the author being a professional writer. The only problem is that it is often hard to find the really relevant and significant information that is hidden in the hundreds of pages of text.

E. A. Sloane, *Sloane's Bicycle Maintenance Manual.* Simon and Schuster, New York.

A comprehensive maintenance and repair manual by the same author. Quite complete, though often hard to follow and lacking in practical approach. Just the same, a worthwhile book to look up some of the things you don't find answered elsewhere.

Sutherland, Hart, Allen, *Sutherland's Handbook for Bicycle Mechanics.* Sutherland Publications, Berkeley (CA).

A very expensive loose-leaf collection of otherwise hard-to-find information, ranging from spoke lengths to screw threading and from dimensional standards to interchangeability guides for many components. Don't buy a copy yourself: just make sure your bike shop orders this book, and keep on good terms, so you can refer to it whenever you have a difficult problem.

R. Van der Plas, *Roadside Bicycle Repairs.* Bicycle Books, San Francisco.

Not merely an abridged version of the present book, but one written specifically to help you carry out emergency repairs by the roadside with a minimum of tools. Small enough to take along, yet adequate for just about any job you can carry out yourself with simple tools.

R. Van der Plas, *The Mountain Bike Book.* Bicycle Books, San Francisco.

The first, and so far the most complete, book devoted entirely to the new breed of fat-tire bicycles. The technical advice and repair instructions in this book are restricted entirely to those applicable to mountain bikes. An essential addition for the bike book library, since the maintenance of these bikes is not sufficiently covered in most of the other repair manuals.

Troubleshooting Guide

Problem/symptom	Possible cause	Required correction	For description see page
tiring position	1. incorrect saddle adjustment	adjust saddle	19, 38
	2. incorrect handlebar adjustment	adjust handlebars	19, 30
	3. incorrect stem extension length	replace stem	31
	4. incorrect frame size	replace bike or frame	
high resistance (when coasting or pedalling)	1. tire rubs on frame or accessory	adjust or straighten	wheel: 85 frame: 25f accessory: 113ff
	2. wheel bearings out of adjustment	adjust and lubricate	81
	3. insufficient tire pressure	inflate/fix puncture	93
	4. wheel bent or loose	straighten and fasten	80, 85
high resistance (when pedalling only)	1. chain dirty, worn or unlubricated	clean, lubricate, replace	50
	2. bottom bracket bearings out of adjustment	adjust, lubricate, overhaul or replace	41ff
	3. pedal bearings out of adjustment	adjust, lubricate, replace	57
	4. chain or chainwheel rubs on frame or accessory	straighten or replace, correct chain line	chainwheel 49, 52 accessory 113ff
tire or other part rubs against frame or accessory	1. see above	see above	
bike pulls to one side	1. wheels misaligned	adjust, center and align	78ff
	2. front fork bent	replace or straighten	36

Symptom	Cause	Remedy	Page
	3. head-set damaged	overhaul or replace	32ff
	4. frame out of alignment	straighten or replace	25ff
bike vibrates (especially when coasting fast)	1. wheels misaligned	adjust and align	78ff
	2. wheel bearings loose	adjust	81
	3. head-set out of adjustment	adjust, overhaul or replace	34
disturbing noises while pedalling	1. chainwheel, crank or pedal loose	fasten or replace	45ff, 57f
	2. chain seriously dry, dirty or worn	clean, lubricate or replace	49ff
	3. bottom bracket bearing or pedal bearing out of adjustment	adjust, lubricate, overhaul	41ff, 57
chain jumps or slips	1. new chain on worn sprocket (derailleur or non-derailleur bike)	replace sprocket or entire freewheel	52ff
	2. chain far worn or loose (non-derailleur bike)	adjust chain tension or replace	50
	3. stiff or bent chain link	replace link or chain	50
chain drops off chainwheel or sprocket	1. derailleur out of adjustment (derailleur bike)	adjust derailleurs	62, 66
	2. chain loose or worn (non-derailleur bike)	adjust or replace chain	50
	3. chainwheel bent or loose	straighten or tighten	49f
	4. incorrect chain line	correct chain line	52
irregular pedalling movement	1. crank, bottom bracket or pedal loose	adjust or tighten	41ff, 45f, 56ff
	2. pedal axle or crank bent	straighten or replace	45f, 57

Problem/symptom	Possible cause	Required correction	For description see pages
derailleur gears do not engage properly	1. derailleur out of adjustment	adjust derailleur	62, 66
	2. derailleur dirty or damaged	overhaul derailleur	64, 68
	3. derailleur control lever or cable damaged, corroded or maladjusted	clean, lubricate, adjust or replace	64f, 68f
	4. chain too short or too long	correct or replace	49f
	5. cable guides or lever attachment loose	tighten	68
	6. (front) derailleur loose or not straight	tighten and align	66f
indexed derailleur does not shift properly	1. cable damaged or corroded	replace and lubricate	64f
	2. derailleur out of adjustment	adjust derailleur	65f
hub gearing does not work properly	1. hub out of adjustment	adjust hub gear	73f
	2. shift lever defective	clean, lubricate or replace	75ff
	3. control cable pinched or defective	free, lubricate or replace	75
	4. cable guide loose	re-position and tighten	75
rim brake ineffective	1. brake out of adjustment	adjust brake	101
	2. rim wet, greasy or dirty	clean rim	22
	3. steel rim in wet weather	replace by aluminum rim	84, 86
	4. brake cable corroded, pinched or damaged	free, lubricate or replace cable	103f
	5. handle loose or damaged	tighten, free, lubricate or replace	104
	6. wheel seriously out of round	straighten rim	85
	7. brake loose or bent	tighten, free, lubricate or replace	101ff

Symptom	Cause	Remedy	Page
rim brake jitters	1. brake loose	tighten	105f
	2. rim seriously out of round	straighten rim	85
	3. rim dirty or greasy	clean rim	22
	4. head-set loose	adjust head-set	34
rim brake squeals	1. brake pad contacts rim poorly	adjust or bend	102
	2. rim dirty	clean rim	22
	3. brake pad worn or dirty	replace brake pad	102
	4. brake arms loose	tighten pivot bolt	105ff
	(if none of these: don't worry, it's not serious)		
coaster brake ineffective	1. chain loose	adjust chain	50
	2. brake counter-lever loose	tighten	111
	3. brake hub defective	overhaul or replace hub	111
hub brake ineffective	1. cable or control problems	see under rim brake	110
	2. brake counter-lever loose	tighten lever	110
	3. brake lining worn or greasy	reline brake segments	110
stirrup brake ineffective	1. control rod or lever problems	check, straighten, lubricate and adjust control rods	112
	2. brake pads worn or rim problems	as for rim brake	
generator lighting defective	1. bulb defective	replace bulb	114
	2. wiring contact loose	repair connection	114f
	3. contact in lamp housing defective	repair contact	114f

Details of Your Bicycle

General
Make: . . . .
Type: . . . .
Year: . . . .

Frame No.: . . . .
Size: . . . .
Color: . . . .

Frame
Make: . . . .
Height: . . . .
Length/wheel base: . . . .
Head tube angle: . . . .
Seat tube angle: . . . .
Tubing: . . . .
Weight: . . . .
Remarks: . . . .

Wheels
Tire type: . . . .
Tire size: . . . .
Valve type: . . . .
Rim type: . . . .
Rim size: . . . .
Rim material: . . . .
Spoke size: . . . .
No. of spokes: . . . .
Hub make: . . . .
Threading rear hub: . . . .
Remarks: . . . .

Steering
Head-set: . . . .
Thread type: . . . .
Head tube length: . . . .
Fork rake: . . . .
Bar extension size: . . . .
Bar diameter: . . . .
Bar type: . . . .
Remarks: . . . .

Crank-set
Bottom bracket make: . . . .
Thread type: . . . .
Axle length: . . . .
Crank length: . . . .
Cotter pin size: . . . .
Remarks: . . . .

Saddle
Make: . . . .
Type: . . . .

Pedals
Make: . . . .

Seat post make: ....

Seat post diameter: ....

Remarks: ....

Brakes

Type: ....

Make: ....

Model: ....

Size: ....

Brake pads: ....

Cables: ....

Remarks: ....

Lighting

Type: ....

Make F/R: ....

Bulbs F/R: ....

Batteries F/R: ....

Remarks: ....

Gear table

Type: ....

Treading: ....

Toeclips: ....

Remarks: ....

Front derailleur

Make: ....

Type: ....

Capacity: ....

Remarks: ....

Rear derailleur

Make: ....

Type: ....

Capacity: ....

Remarks: ....

Chain wheels

Make: ....

Sizes: ....

Hole pattern: ....

Material: ....

Remarks: ....

Freewheel/sprockets

Make: ....

Threading: ....

Sprocket sizes: ....

Remarks: ....

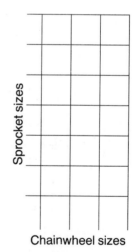

Sprocket sizes

Chainwheel sizes

Screw Threading Standards

Thread location	BCI-standard[1] (English)	ISO-standard[5] (French)	Italian	USA[2]
Bottom bracket fixed cup (right side)	1.370 x 24 TPI (L)	35 x 1 mm (R)	36 mm x 24 TPI-F (R)	
Bottom bracket adj. cup (left side)	1.370 x 24 TPI (R)	35 x 1 mm (R)	36 mm x 24 TPI-F (R)	
Pedal (left)	9⁄16" x 20 TPI (L)	14 x 1.25 mm (L)	BCI-standard	½" x 20 TPI (L)
Pedal (right)	9⁄16" x 20 TPI (R)	14 x 1.25 mm (R)	BCI-standard	½" x 20 TPI (R)
Head-set	1.000 x 24 TPI	25 x 1 mm	1.000 x 24 TPI-F	1" x 24 TPI
Freewheel	1.370 x 24 TPI	34.7 x 1 mm	35 mm x 24 TPI	(English)
Derailleur attachment	(French)	10 x 1 mm	10 mm x 26 TPI	(French)

Remarks

1. Applies to quality bicycles with BSA cranks only. Some major manufacturers do not adhere to any of these standards for their cheapest models, which may be equipped with Ashtabula cranks if American built. Raleigh uses a variant of the BCI system on some of its lower priced models. See *Sutherland's Handbook for Bicycle Mechanics* for more extensive details.
2. The American standards only apply to simple bicycles with Ashtabula crankset (consequently no data for bottom bracket threading are given). Quality bicycles made in the USA generally conform to English standards.
3. Country of origin does not necessarily coincide with the particular standards used. Except for French and Italian bicycles, most models imported into the USA have English standard components. For more details see *Sutherland's Handbook for Bicycle Mechanics.*
4. On many French bikes the derailleur lug has a 9 mm unthreaded hole, which may have to be tapped to the appropriate standard.
5. Old ISO-standard. The proposed future standard differs in several respects, but is not yet in force.

Index

Ordering books published by Bicycle Books, Inc.

Fill out coupon and send to:

Bicycle Books, Inc.
PO Box 2038
Mill Valley CA 94941 (USA)
FAX (415) 381 6912

Please include payment in full (check or money order made out to Bicycle Books, Inc.). If not paid in advance, books will be sent UPS COD.

Please send the following books:

Title	copies @	price	=	$
The Mountain Bike Book	____ copies @	$9.95	=	$ _____
The Bicycle Repair Book	____ copies @	$8.95	=	$ _____
The Bicycle Racing Guide	____ copies @	$10.95	=	$ _____
The Bicycle Touring Manual	____ copies @	$10.95	=	$ _____
Roadside Bicycle Repairs	____ copies @	$4.95	=	$ _____
Major Taylor (hardcover)	____ copies @	$19.95	=	$ _____
Bicycling Fuel	____ copies @	$7.95	=	$ _____
Mountain Bike Maintenance	____ copies @	$7.95	=	$ _____
In High Gear	____ copies @	$10.95	=	$ _____
The Bicycle Fitness Book	____ copies @	$7.95	=	$ _____
The Bicycle Commuting Book	____ copies @	$7.95	=	$ _____
The New Bike Book	____ copies @	$4.95	=	$ _____
Bicycle Technology	____ copies @	$16.95	=	$ _____
The Tour of the Forest Bike Race	____ copies @	$9.95	=	$ _____

Sub total $ _____
California residents add sales tax $ _____
Shipping and handling: $2.50 first book,
$1.00 each additional book (within US) $ _____

Total amount $ _____

Name _____   All prices quoted are US $
Address _____
City, _____
State, zip _____   Tel. (____) _____
MC / VISA No. _____   X _____